CONFUSION TO PEACE

Published by Spines
ISBN: 979-8-89569-113-7

CONFUSION TO PEACE

A MEMOIR BY MARVIN ALEXANDER FORD

MARVIN ALEXANDER FORD

My title is somewhat of an Oxymoron. Two words that contradict how they are written in my title. Although it is a perfectly detailed depiction of my life. I lived in total confusion from my beginning and up to my adult years.

All the way to the truth coming out who my father was. From that point on, I experienced total peace.

CONTENTS

PART FOUR
TRANQUILITY

DEDICATION

To my brother and sister:
Rason Ford Tesha Ford

In loving memory of my siblings:
Larry Ford Freddie Ford
Deborah Ford Cutchin

In loving memory of my father:
Lester "Bob" Ford

In loving memory of my mom:
Evelyn King Jack, I owe everything to you mom
/grandmother.

You will never be forgotten; I appreciate all that you have.
done for me in my young beginning.

PROLOGUE

My story begins at my conception, then subsequently my birth. A path of denial and confusion occurs. That would go on for decades. The effects of the decision my birth mother made hurt me deeply. After being dropped off at my grandmother's home. She went on to become my mom forever.

Being without a dad was very tough in my whole existence. I wouldn't find this out until I was around fifty years old. After confessing the truth, my birth mother did a complete 180 degrees of denial.

This story will chronicle my life from birth to adulthood. The early years were filled with obstacles of many varieties. Such as dealing with the Jim Crow laws. Which didn't end in the state of Louisiana until the early to mid-1970s. The confusion about who was my father. Why did my sister and brother have fathers, and I did not? The difference between my birth mother and my mom. It was a lot to handle for a young child.

Had to deal with my cousin next door to us. Got bullied a lot, because they knew I had no father. My mom marries the father of her two youngest sons (my two uncles). Who hated me from the very start (my step-grandfather I guess)? So much so, that once he told me to get rid of my dog. I was eight years old, and of course, I couldn't. So, one day he called me outside to a little wooded area near our home. He had my dog tied to a tree by the neck. As I stood there watching in total horror. He picked up a shovel looking right at me with a mean look. I stood there frozen, in total confusion. Surely, he's not going to hit my dog…If so, why? He killed my dog with that shovel, right in front of me. Then he violently threw the shovel at me and told me to bury my dog. On another occasion, my step-grand-father and I were standing together outside the back door. My mom was speaking to him. I was lost in a daydream and not paying attention.

Evidently, she must have called my name several times and finally, I responded with a yell (WHAT!!!). I never saw it coming. He slapped me so hard that I almost blacked out. I was lying flat on the ground and barely heard my mom tell him that if he ever hit me like that again, she would kill him.

We lived on a small farm, in a house that had no running water, and no bathrooms, we used what they referred to as a "pot," to be used at night. Then it would be emptied in the morning (my job). That would be the outhouse, for emptying and using the rest room.

My mom died just before I turned ten years old. This and many other factors may explain why I had to repeat the fifth grade. Why have I wet the bed for almost eleven years? Why I was so quiet and almost never talked? The school years were a blur. The only thing that got me through them was sports. After my mom died, my birth mother moved in. She continued to not tell me who my father was. So, I was never at home. I just needed to get through the indignation I had toward her.

The neighborhood experience will be not unlike "The Little Rascals" TV show from long ago. My high school years bothered me. If I could, I would go back and do better than I did… effort-wise. I couldn't wait to get out of Louisiana. As soon as I could, I joined the US Navy. In 1979 while still a senior in high school. Took off for boot camp in August of 1980.

My first marriage failed unceremoniously. With that being said, I still got to raise three wonderful children, adopted or not. Lost my daughter at the age of sixteen years old to suicide (depression). My children did so much good to my life, that it overshadowed all the negatives. Getting them was the best thing I could have ever done. My current wife made me whole.

I once aspired to be a stockbroker, while working in the real estate industry part-time. By accident, I stumbled onto the world of trucking, and it was the best occupation for me. I believe that even if I had graduated from Harvard University, I would still be a trucker. Truck driving is therapeutic and a life-rewarding experience.

When I found out who my father was, it completed me in a roundabout way. My birth mother had sex with her sister's husband (my aunt and uncle), and they produced me. My birth mother considered having an abortion (abortions weren't legal in 1961). She didn't do it only because of the cost. My birth mother never gave me the opportunity to see him alive like my father (I knew him as my uncle). My father died at the age of 60 in 1990. I have totally forgiven my birth mother. I don't judge her, since I am not perfect or without sin. I call my 89-year-old birth mother all the time and talk mostly about the bible. I pray that she repents all her sins. I am at complete peace today and beyond.

AFTERWARDS

On November 16, 1961, I was born at 5 pm Thursday in the evening. My birth mother was all alone, because of the circumstance leading up to this birth of mine. Approximately nine months earlier, I was conceived in complete controversy. Basically, my mother got impregnated by her sister's husband with me being the finished product.

I eventually was dumped off at my grandmother's house by my birth mother. I would remain there until my grandmother's death. Just before I turned ten years old. My birth mother took my two half-siblings with her and left me behind. They did this sort of thing back then when an embarrassing thing happened in a family. They would keep it a dark family secret forever if possible. Examples of these things would be unplanned pregnancies, rapes, incest…etcetera.

The early years of my life were loaded with many

things. Growing up with my mom, I learned so much. In these early years, my mom and all the adults around us had to deal with the Jim Crow Laws. I had little to no knowledge of these racist laws. The adults in our community kept all of us kids away from it all. We simply never went to town to even see things like, "One water fountain for Whites and one separate Fountain for Colored. We lived in an all-Afro-American community, and only saw Caucasian People at School as Teachers.

When I was old enough to start wondering about my existence. While living with my grandmother, who I referred to as my mom. I started questioning who that lady was who could visit from time to time. Calling herself my mother, but never sticking around long enough to bond. Later, I came to realize she was my birth mother. I was so confused for many years. I did not seriously start asking my birth mother who my father was until age ten years old. My mom raised me better than I could have expected. Under the circumstances, I was lucky to have been with my mom. I wasn't wanted by my birth mother for reasons I would not know about for many years. The early part of my life was very confusing. My half- brother and half-sister (different dads for all three of us), got to live with our birth mother for a reason. To avoid scandal and fall out from how I came to be.

My real mom (my grandmother) was my hero. She was always there for me. She was not an educated woman. Born in the year 1908, a time of great danger for our people. She was done having children by the year 1944 at 36 years old. My mom was 53 years old when I was dropped off on her. By my birth mother and of course, her mother. She would only live for a little over nine years, after my arrival. My mom died at the age of 61 years old. I often wonder if that had that had something to do with me. She was not in good health, due to miscellaneous illnesses. All I'll say to my birth mother is why put my mom through this? Why not live the truth and tell it as it happened? I would have defended her vehemently.

I grew up next to my Aunt Dorothy and Uncle Lawrance and all my cousins. These kids were many in number. A lot happened between us over the years. To complicate things for me, my mom marries my two younger uncles' father (my step-grandfather). This man hated me from the beginning, He was to become my enemy. We basically lived on a little mini farm. It was so much more.

The early school years for me weren't unbearable at all. My Life to this point was very confusing. My rock (my mom) kept me on the straight and narrow. I Had plenty of opportunities to become a bad kid. I got through school okay, but I did not do as well as I could. The mess involving my birth mom had something to do with it. When I got to the fifth grade, I struggled badly. It was the last year before I lost my rock. She died and I failed the fifth grade and had to repeat.

My birth mother moves in upon the death of my real mom. The good thing was the fact that my enemy moved out. I became rebellious during this transition. I begged my birth mother to tell me who my father was. All I got from her was Lies. I spent more time at my best friend's house than at home.

This happened all the way through school. I played lots of sports and messed around in the neighborhood. Sports and staying away from home gave me an out. It was too stressful at home for me. After high school, I couldn't wait to get out of Louisiana. I joined the US Navy and left for good.

My first marriage produced three beautiful children for us. I devoted my life to my children. I didn't want what I went through to happen to them in any way. My kids refreshed me and gave me purpose in life.

My second wife made me complete. She and I are like soulmates. It's been a roller coaster ride, but isn't life like that for us all? My birth mother finally came clean on who my father was. Then quickly went on to deny it again. It is an absolute shame to not have had the opportunity to meet my dad as my dad. I was around him many times when I was younger, as was my uncle. Yes, my father is my aunt's husband, the sister of my birth mother. My father died in 1990, but little did I know I had a younger sister and brother. I also found out that my three cousins were really my siblings.

I became a truck driver by accident. What

happened was that a friend needed help with hauling Air Freight to LAX (Los Angeles International Airport from San Diego, California) cargo facilities. I had gotten out of the Navy to take on my Twin baby boys. I did Real Estate for some time until I decided to finish my college degree. Trucking just happened and I really was a natural at it. I liked it so much; that I'd do it over anything else.

I lost my beloved daughter to suicide at age sixteen and that got to me. I never got over it, neither will I ever. She and I were close, but depression won. Depression is a real killer. I still have my twin sons and two other adult kids. The twins are in the US Navy and doing great. My younger two kids are in college, and doing great. Overall, I am blessed in the wake of my tremendously lost and confusing childhood.

I've had numerous near-death (close calls) experiences in my life. But I don't worry about death. I worry about being able to live in the moment.

Being able to have been all over the world is special to me. Having the chance to have traveled to every state in the United States is unique in itself.

PART ONE
ODOR OF MENDACITY
(UNTRUTHFULNESS; TENDENCY TO LIE)

CHAPTER 1
THE ACT OF MY CONCEPTION

To eliminate any questions about the validity of who my father really is. I did a DNA test, and it is confirmed. It finally can rest on all the lies, doubt, and denial.

The act of my conception occurred sometime in January 1961. My birth mother (Melba) had sex with my future uncle/father (Lester) on this date. My uncle was married to my maternal aunt (Bernadine). Who was my birth mother's sister? The pregnancy brought my birth mother a large degree of disgrace from family members. She was made to live in a one-room shack behind my aunt Dorothy's house. This caused a rift in the family that was very intense.

My very pregnant birth mother has a lot to deal with during this tumultuous period. This is a serious punishment for a heinous act. My father just went on living a family life as if nothing happened (He was probably unaware until much later). Back then, a bread winner got a lot more leeway. Back in the day, if there were a rape or incest, families would keep it a secret forever if necessary. My conception was a consensual act; however, an act of betrayal between siblings. One day my birth mother (while pregnant with me, encountered a snake. In Louisiana, we have many varied species of snakes. Many are poisonous, but in this instance, it was not determined the type of snake she encountered. The story is still told around my family, to this day in a hushed tone. The snake was the symbol for this devilish act of my conception. My Aunt Bernadine, my father's wife, always loved me and saw me as an innocent child. My people were very superstitious back then, which is probably why my birth mother said it was a sign of some type. This story still comes up every now and then. Again, Louisiana is a Voodoo-practicing state, they believed in it strongly back then at least. I am grateful for this snake not interfering with her pregnancy with me.

Unfortunately, I was considered a bastard child. This was done to protect my father's family and to bury the truth (To this day it is unknown when my father finally found out about me). After I was born on November 16· 1961. My birth mother couldn't wait to get out of town. Shortly after my birth, I was dropped off at my grandmother's house, and subsequently abandoned. This is the moment when my grandmother (Evelyn) became my MOM! My uncle (Uncle Hebert) was 17 years old and still in high school. He was also living with my mom, his mother. Before he passed away in the early 2000s, he was the second person to tell me that Lester Ford was my father. My brother Freddy was the first to tell me who my father was. He along with my other two siblings on my Aunt Bernadine (their mother) before her passing. She said, "Marvin is not just your first cousin, he is also your brother.

My aunt Dorothy, who lives next door to us refused to take a baby picture of me. This aunt always treated me badly from the beginning. She evidently had a serious problem with how I came to be. I started noticing at an early age how badly she treated my birth mother when my birth mother would visit. This aunt eventually ended up taking my picture at 6 months old, along with her son Darrell. This turned out to be the only baby picture that was ever taken. My next picture wouldn't take place until I was in, "Head Start" (now known as pre-school).

Many people know about this sinful act of how I was brought into this world. I am grateful for being here on this earth. I am also grateful to have been raised by my mom (grandmother). Nevertheless, no one ever came forward until I was almost 50 years old. My uncle Hebert, who was in high school at the time was dropped off. My favorite aunt Bernadine, was married to my father. Told her kids (my siblings: Deborah, Larry, and Freddy) who my father was. She died shortly after telling her kids. I was at a university of Norte Dame college football game. When I heard of my favorite aunt Bernadine's death. I took my twin boys with me down to Houston, Texas (by car) for my aunt's funeral. This was when I found out who my father was from my three siblings before Uncle Hebert would eventually tell me. I would drive all the way to Houston from Chicago and back to Chicago from Houston non-stop. My twin boys had perfect attendance and I aimed to keep it perfect. It was important to me and them equally.

-Year O the Ox-

"If you were born in 1961 (and two other years) then you're an Ox.

Your personality could be characterized as hard working in the background, intelligent, and reliable but you do not need praise."

Quoted from "Chinese New Year, net on February 13, 2021

-Hit Music in 1961_
(Billboard year-end top R&B singles of 1961)

"It's gonna work out fine." By Ike and tina Turner-
"Shop around." By The Miracles-
"Stand by Me." By Ben E. King-

"Every beat of my heart." By Glady's Knight and the PiPs- "Baby you're right." By James Brown-

"Hit the road jack." By Ray Charles- "At last." By Etta James-

"Pony time." By Chubby Checker-

"Please Mr. postman." By The Marvelettes-

My Uncle Hebert finished high school and left for San Francisco, California. Now it's just my mom and me. My birth mother is still missing in action at this point. Kinda don't blame her in a way, but I'm still confused with it all. My Uncle Hebert moves in with his father (my future step-grandfather) in San Francisco, California. His father will eventually move in with my mom and me, He is another one who showed hatred toward me because of how I came to be.

I was the only kid in our neighborhood without a father. From as far back as I can remember, I noticed who all had fathers. Thinking back to my early years, I was a quiet baby. I was almost unnoticed by neighbors and visitors. I can remember getting caught trying to stick a wire into an electrical outlet, by my mom. I felt a slight shock, just as my mom was kicking the wire that I was holding out of my hand. She saved my life in an instant. I can remember running into my birth mother's stomach, right after she had had surgery. I was only two years old and happy to see her. She screamed out in pain and scared me. My birth mother was ok after being run into by me, as the story goes. All I know is that I was so happy to see her. I was young when I remembered walking to the outhouse to use the restroom. Yes, I was a quiet kid, but I really picked up everything I heard.

As I observed the adults talking. Back then, children were to only speak when spoken to.

During another visit from my birth mother, I saw my half-sister (Paula) for the first time. At least that is the way I remember it. We went out for food to eat. It is my half-sister, my birth mother, and my half-sister's father (Hardy Edwards). Imagine how I felt seeing that both my half-sister and half- brother (Billy) had fathers. Around this time, I began to question my birth mother about who my father was. This is when the lies begin. I was around the age of five years old. Calling Paula and Billy my half-brother and sister because it is accurate. We all three share the same birth mother, but all have different fathers. With mine being the only one that is unknown. Later, I see Billy for the first time, he is ten years older than I am. Paula is only one year younger than I. We all were given the same last name (Alexander).

That name came from my half-brother's father (Joseph Alexander). My birth mother (Melba) explained to me that she had no choice but to name Paula and me Alexander. Melba told me that she tried to give me her maiden name (King). They allegedly told her that she had to use her married name. Even though she had been separated from her husband (Billy's dad, Joseph Alexander) for almost ten years. My last name is not correct because of this, neither is Paula's maiden name. We should have been at least named King for our last name. Since I didn't find out who my father was until around fifty years old, checkmate. I was basically stuck with Alexander for good. I consider myself to be a Ford and no one can change that. I thought of maybe changing my last name once I retire to my rightful name of Ford. My half-siblings lived with my birth mother, which I never understood, growing up. Now I understand it very well. I can't totally blame Melba on the one hand, but on the other hand, I do. I had a good upbringing in my mom's home (where I would live my entire childhood until age eighteen years old). I still feel robbed of having a personal relationship with my father.

I know what happened between my birth mother and father was consensual sex, which resulted in my existence today. But I thought the article below was remarkably interesting. No, what they did was not incest at all, but it sure feels that way in my mind. As I look at it today. Especially since my birth mother told me that she considered an abortion for her pregnancy with me. People wonder why I'm so strongly against abortion. This is one of the reasons. "Adult on-adult family incest is often portrayed as consensual incest. It has been sensationalized in the media in shows like (The Game of thrones and Gossip Girl) portraying siblings in seemingly consensual sexual relationships" Quoted from Incest awake (Our Alliance).

Although my birth parents had consensual sex, it did produce me. It was an adulterous act against my aunt Bernadine. My father's wife and mother's sister were the injured person. Their marriage never fully recovered.

Everyone made the truth go away for decades. One thing my mom taught me was to never lie. When growing up with her, lying wasn't even tolerated. It bothers me to this day when I even hear someone lying. To this very day, people deny the truth about who my father is. Unfortunately, my father is no longer with us. He passed away in 1990, the year I got out of the US Navy after ten years of service. I didn't find out who my father was until twenty years after his death. Rest in peace, my father! This is an incredibly sad deal and so very unnecessary. Guess it was just not meant to be. It gives me peace to know that my father spoke of me to my younger siblings and second wife Brenda.

CHAPTER 2

ABORTION CLOSE CALL

On the second confession by my birth mother. She informed me who my father was. Later, she denied it again, for good, I'm sure. Nevertheless, while listening to this confession, she brings up abortion. She admitted to me that when she found out she was pregnant with me, abortion was an option. Melba was unapologetic, showing zero remorse. All I could think at this point was how extremely lucky I was to even exist. My birth mother went on to explain how they went behind my Aunt Bernadine (Melba's sister) back for sex. Abortions were not legal in 1961, so it would have been a crime. If my birth mother had the money to go through with aborting her pregnancy...she would have in a heartbeat. I forgave my birth mother 100%. We talk on the phone from time to time and quote the Bible a lot.

Yes, what they have done (my birth mother and

father) was an immoral act. I'm just glad to be here alive and well in spite of this act. I'm proud to be pro-life and will debate anyone on this barbaric act known as abortion.

My poor grandmother (mom) raised me to be God-fearing, law-abiding and a productive citizen of society with strong morals and values. She gave me the core principles and values that have made me the man I am today. I Can't imagine what she went through watching over me. She taught me how to make pancakes and some other smaller kitchen tasks. I would get up in the morning and get on my knees to pray. I then had to empty all the pots (no bathroom or running water) into the outhouse. Our outhouse was about thirty yards behind our home. Then deal with the sheets that I wet every night. I was a bedwetter for several years. One day I stopped at a youthful age (probably around ten years old). "Psychological or Emotional problems: Emotional stress caused by traumatic events or disruptions in your normal routine can cause bedwetting. For example, moving to a new home, enrolling in a new school, the death of a loved one or sexual abuse may cause bedwetting episodes," (January 20, 2023) quoted from http://my.clevelandclinic.org>health. As I alluded to earlier, I was confused and could have been affected by psychological issues. Like the similar symptoms described in the quoted information from the Cleveland clinic. I was never diagnosed with a reason for my bedwetting. I was a kid with some issues brought on by all that had happened to me from birth onward. Being dropped off and abandoned by my birth mother had a mental effect on me. It was a traumatic and emotional time for me. I think that there were too many correlating facts to rule out. Could It have been physical? Like an undersized bladder or another urinary issue? All I know is that I was a bedwetter as a young child. It caused a tremendous amount of embarrassment.

CHAPTER 3

THE EARLY YEARS

Part of my chores was to go get water from my aunt Bernadine's house. The same house that my father resided at. They lived just two houses down from our home. That is how we got our drinking and other use water. Taking baths, washing dishes, and drinking water were some of the uses. My mom gave me some challenging tasks to perform daily. I never complained for some reason. I did the dishes and helped with the weekly house cleaning. We never missed a week unless my mom was not feeling well.

My mom sold many household goods, like eggs, Fudge bars, peanut patties candy bars, popcorn balls, pies, frozen cups, and candy apples. On one such sale of eggs, I have seen a Caucasian person for the first time in my life (a lady and her young child). I just remembered staring at them both in complete amazement.

My mom made her own soap, or soap with Lye in its ingredients. She used it to wash clothes by hand. "Before people could get their hands on processed sodium hydroxide, they had to make lye the old-fashioned way by leaching water through wood ashes layered in a barrel or some other container. The result was primarily a soft, gooey soap. Wood ashes have a tendency to produce mostly potassium hydroxide." Quoted the spruce crafts https://www.thesprucecrafts.com.

Like I said many times before, my mom was uneducated with advanced smarts. I am sure there are many more things she did that I was not aware of. My cousins who lived next door to us influenced my life to a certain extent. Until I moved out of Louisiana for good. "I DON'T KNOW THEM AND THEY KNOW NOT ME," meaning there is no relationship between us anymore. My cousin's mother (my aunt Dorothy) hated me from day one because of the circumstances of my birth. Events that occurred between my birth mother and my father angered a lot of people in the family. Once, my cousin Darrell (who was closest to my age) took my bike when I told him not to. When he came back, I slapped him in the face. This caused him to cry and run to his house to tell his mother. I put my bike back away and began to finish my supper. My aunt Dorothy came over and threatened me with corporal punishment. I didn't care about her threat, and she knew. I told her that if he took my bike again, I would hit him again. She marched away showing lots of indignation toward me. I respectfully returned the same to her.

My cousin Michael (three years older than me) beat me up once after a car ride. I fell asleep on his leg; at some point, I drooled on him as I slept. I told my aunt Dorothy what happened, and she actually smiled. She did nothing about what her son had done to me. After a while, I stopped going to her for anything.

Incidentally, my aunt Dorothy didn't hate my birth mother (Melba).

She was very mean to her and treated her rudely. It bothered me how mean she was to my birth mother, right in front of me. Both my half-sister and I showed indignation with our birth mother for allowing it. The only positive thing to come from my next-door cousins was my uncle Lawrence. He was somewhat of a father figure to me in a small way. Uncle Lawrance had a house full of children to deal with. I was on the back burner, which is understandable.

One day I was walking home from school, in total solitude. While passing in front of Reginal's house, Reginal motioned me over (Reginal was a year behind me as I was in the first grade). He asked me if I would play with him. I thought about it for a second and finally said yes. I literally got beat up the whole time I was there. Once I got home with a torn shirt which led to a whipping by way of a switch (a small tree limb minus its leaves). Down south, switches were used a lot for discipline and child-rearing. The effects of this small tree limb are still green for strengthening and toughness. A form of corporal punishment that works to perfection. The very next day while passing by Reginal's house, I anticipated another invitation to play. I was rewarded when Reginal asked if I would play with him again. It wasn't really playing, but more like fighting. I got the best of him this time and felt much better. After the beating that I received the previous day, where my mom had told me "To not let that boy beat you up again." That was her way of giving me permission to fight to protect my honor. When I got home, my mom said nothing, since my clothes were not damaged. If my clothes had been damaged, I would have been punished for sure. After my second fight, Reginal and I became very good friends. We never ever had a fight of any kind to this very day.

Reginal passed away years ago and was an incredibly good friend of mine to end.

Shortly after this period, I became friends with Patrick Citizen. A friendship that would start in 1967 and continues to this very day. Patrick is like a brother to me. I would be at his family's home all the time, growing up. Especially when I was staying away from home during the years following my mom's death. After my mom passed away, my birth mother moved in and that was an issue. Which was the dilemma about who my father was. Patrick's family took me in like I was one of them. To this day, I believe in my heart that the Citizen's saved me. Without them, I could have gone on a different path in life. I love them all and basically learn many life lessons from them.

Gilbert Harrison bullied me so many times. I lost count of how many times Gilbert repeated grades prior to high school. He was a lot older than I and much bigger than I. I'm guessing at least three to four years older.

Nevertheless, we were in the same grade for many years. I never complained to anyone about him because I wasn't that type of kid.

I was also bullied by Tommy Rigmaiden, who was even older than Gilbert. For instance, one day a group of us same-aged boys were walking down the street. Tommy and many of his much older friends were playing street basketball together. There were about six of us, but I was the only one without a father (Yes that made a difference). A kid without a mother or a father was a target. As we started to pass by their game playing, Tommy motions me over (With a "Hey little Nigger, get over here). He allows my friends to leave, and they do. Tommy then conveys to me that he has the wrong shoes for playing basketball. Then he asked me what size sneakers I had on. I told him because I knew if I did not, he would have just ripped them off and hit me. So, he makes me take off my sneakers and keep an eye on his shoes while he plays basketball. I had to stay there waiting for him to finish his game, so he could give me my sneakers back. It was almost dark when he finished. Which meant I was late. When I got home, I got a whipping. Several times after that experience took place, there were repeated instances. There weren't many streets in our neighborhood safe from bullies. Seemingly older kids that knew I was a prime game with no father. I don't believe my birth mother either knew or cared about these issues that I delt with on a regular basis. I was bullied at school at times, while my mom was still alive. But I handled those by fighting or keeping it to myself. They were usually short in duration. Basically, the bullying ended right there in each instance. In the third grade, a kid two years older than me bullied me. Another one was with Jimmy in the sixth grade. He wasn't bullying, but more like harassing me. A very irritating kid that thought he was more than he was.

My aunt Dorothy (next door aunt) took my birthday gift I got from my aunt Florence once. As I stood there in gleeful anticipation waiting for my gift to be handed to me. My aunt Florence pulled out this very long string of attached individual bubble gum balls (out of her purse). Just as she was handing it over to me, my aunt Dorothy yanked them out of my hands violently. She went on to explain to me that I wasn't getting them all. She started handing them out to all the other kids who were lingering around.

Kids that were her own and some of the neighborhood kids. I hated her as I took off running. I stopped at our out house and cried hard. My enemy had struck again. I vowed to never eat any of the bubble gum…and I did not. I secretly wanted my aunt Dorothy to die (thank God that never happened as she is now in her 90s). On another occasion involving my aunt Dorothy.

This time it was an omission by design, which my aunt inflicted upon me. She arrived back from a New York trip on which she was visiting my aunt Bernadine. As my aunt Dorothy was seated on the steps of her back door. All of us kids were there waiting impatiently for a toy. It was her kids (my cousins), the neighborhood Kids (Stef, Kevin, Timmy, and others) and I. I was standing directly in front of my aunt (1st in line so to speak). There were kids behind me and on both sides of where I was standing. Probably about ten kids in all. My aunt began to hand out toys to kids behind me and on both sides of where I was standing. I began to realize that she was ignoring me on purpose. Wouldn't you know that she was one toy short? I was the unlucky kid of course. When she handed out the last toy, she looked at me and said no more. I can still hear that remark clearly to this day. I don't remember how long I cried, but it must have been a very long period of time. I woke up the following morning still crying. I have forgiven my aunt Dorothy many years ago and hold nothing against her at all. On the other hand, I feel these words need to be known by whoever has an interest in knowing.

Lying was not allowed in our home. So, when My mom asked me a question, the truth came out automatically. She sent me to Sunday school every Sunday morning (at Pasadena Baptist church). I walked all the way by myself, even at a noticeably youthful age. My mom would show up just before church service began. Somehow my mom always found something on my face that needed attention. She would moisten a handkerchief in her mouth to remove whatever it was from my face. I disliked this, but respecting your elders was a southern thing to be expected.

I was baptized in this oversized jacuzzi-looking pool thing. It terrified me since I did not know how to swim yet. Rev. Thomas (the preacher) held me in this water and then dumbed me under water. To tell you the truth, I got absolutely nothing from any of it. My cousin got baptized that day as well. That helped in a small way. The scene was confusing because of the amount of people surrounding the pool. They were singing a song that sounded like something for a funeral. I survived it all and never thought the same about church again after this traumatizing event. Attending church was not one of my favorite things in life growing up. I have seen/heard people speaking in tongues. People were catching the "Holy Ghost," scaring us kids each time that it occurred. People would stand up without warning and start waving their hands high above their heads and yell things out spontaneously. On the other hand, children had to be quiet (with all that racket going on). If we made a sound, it would probably lead to a whipping later of a quick slap. I never understood any of that.

My cousin Darrell and I were walking home from school one day. Two first graders without a care in the world. It was the winter of 1967. When Darrell and I got to Fourth avenue, we noticed the Clark's dogs were sitting in the middle of the street (Michigan avenue). The dogs were near Fifth avenue, in front of the Clark's house. We both started crying as I stopped walking. Darrell kept walking where the dogs awaited him. I thought after the dogs ate Darrell; they may come to get me. So, I hurried up this embankment leading into the woods (a very thick forest). I found what I thought would be a good hiding place and laid down. I fell asleep in an area about ten feet from the street. I was awakened by my cousins Larry and Freddy (I found out many years later that they were my brothers). They got me and took me home on their bikes. They were my "Knights in Shining Armor" making me feel so safe. I found out later that snow was expected that very night. That was the reason for the big fuss about me. I hate to speculate on if I could have lost my life that night if not found. I am a lucky person in a close call, as I will explain later in this book. Darrell got home unharmed, I guess those big dogs weren't mean after all.

While lying in bed, my heroes (Larry and Freddy) were standing there watching on. My cousin/future sister Deborah is at the foot of my bed with a mischie-vous look on her face. It was a look that I knew all too well, a signal to me that it would be mischief time soon. She and I were close and hung out together all the time. I learned so much from Deborah, Larry, and Freddy and hated that they moved away just a few years later. I wondered if it was because of me.

I must revisit my bedwetting issues that lasted until I was ten years old, at least. It was embarrassing, humiliating, and depressing for me to deal with. The fatherless thing weighed heavily on me, during this period. My early years were a quagmire, to be frank. I believe that I would have been a more well-rounded kid growing up if I had been from a two-parent home. I understand that there are others without a two-parent home who have been successful in life without issues. My situation is odd only because of the many variables involved with my unique situation. i.e., not having birth mom involved in my formative years, not knowing who my father was, and the early death of my mom (grandma) who raised me until the age of 10.

My aunt Bernadine was my favorite aunt. She loved me so much, because of her actions. She was the one who got hurt when I came to be (the circumstances around my birth mother's pregnancy with me). Picture this, my birth mother commits adultery with my aunt's husband. I am conceived from this act. My aunt Berna-dine has an under-two-year-old baby girl (my sister Deborah) to take care of. Not to mention a son who was a toddler (Freddy was under three years old) during this time. My aunt never took it out of me, and I do appreciate her for this. I had enough enemies to deal with throughout my early years. She eventually told her children (my siblings) Larry, Freddy, and Deborah that I was their brother. By way of their father and my birth mother, Melba. Eventually, who I thought were my cousins (Larry, Freddy, and Deborah) explained what their mother had explained to them. We lost all three of them within a two-year period recently. My question is simply why my aunt would have lied about this damaging information. Information that had been locked away as a deep family secret. When my aunt Bernadine died, I lost more than just an aunt. No one else but her could have taken all of this destructive past history and persevered the rest of her life.

I hung out with my then Cousin Deborah the most out of anyone else. She was my playmate, teacher, and best friend. She taught me how to ride a bike, and so much more. The day they left Louisiana for New York City (the Jamaica Queens area) I cried. I believe to my very core that they left because of my existence. Meaning, how I came to be in this world and the act that was committed. Once they were gone, my life got more complicated in dealing with bullying.

One night while going to the outhouse to relieve myself, I got attacked. The Shepherd boys, Pump and Stan did things to me often. Such as shooting me with

BB guns, mostly in my head. On this particular night, I was jumped by Pump Shepherd. As I was leaving the outhouse, on my way back toward our home, Pump knocked me down and started removing my pants and underwear. I didn't know what was going on until I felt his Penis pressing against my Anus area. I then began to fight him as I tried to free myself from his hold on me. Keep in mind that this guy was a teenager, and I was just a little 2nd-grade kid. Because of my relentless fighting against his advance upon me, and the noise I was making. He gave up and let me go. I ran home as fast as I could. Never told my mom are anyone else. If I had told my mom, I feared her killing Pump. Pump never completed the raping of me because I wasn't an easy victim. Meaning, he never penetrated me but was close to doing just that. Stan Shepherd would also shoot me with BB guns and once, years after this hit me so hard in a drill in pee wee football. I believe that I got a concussion from this hit. I got right back up but was dizzy and nauseated for the rest of the day. The headache went on for a couple of weeks. I probably should have gone to get medical attention immediately. One thing was for sure, I was not going to show any weakness after that hit. I popped right back up and protected the little manhood I had at this point in my young life. I am not normally for the death penalty but for any sexual crime done to a child. I say kill them and drop the sexual predator crap.

My aunt Florance was the enforcer's aunt. No one

had the nerve to cross her in any way. She was my babysitter every now and then. I was on my best behavior in her care. I can't think of any incident of Aunt Florance punishing me. My half-sister Paula didn't behave for whatever reason. I mean oh my goodness did she get it. Paula liked to roll her eyes and that was a no- no around Aunt Florence. I loved my aunt Florence since she was always nice to me (probably because of my good behavior or how I came to be?). I was always happy to be around both Aunt Bernadine and Aunt Florance. I spent a lot of time at Aunt Bernadine's house, playing with mostly Deborah. Aunt Florance lived in an apartment right there on the side of Aunt Bernadine's house. Both of my aunts are no longer with us today.

Once, my friend Patrick was hit by a rock, thrown by my cousin Darrell. All the neighborhood kids decided to play a new game. I have no idea why we thought this would be fun. Looking back at this bad Idea, I just cringe. Well, these were the rules, pick teams with an equal number of older and younger kids on each team. Then it was picking weapons, and that would turn out to be "Rocks"! Yes, we were basically going to play hide and seek. One team went and hid, then the other team went to go find them. Whoever got hit with a rock was out. The last kid standing would win it for his team. Much to our chagrin, the game ended almost as soon as it started. Which was probably a good thing (Health wise). Because Patrick, Darrell, and I were together (and on the team opposite the hiding team). For some reason, Darrell decided to throw a rock unexpectedly. Patrick was hit in the back of his head by Darrell's rock. Time froze for what seemed like hours. As Patrick grabbed his injured head. Darrell broke the abyss moment by saying, "Ooh, look at that blood." Patrick had not cried yet, at this point. Until I followed Darrell, with "Sho is"! With that, Patrick saw the blood on his hands and took off for home in a sprint. It must have scared him because he screamed the whole way home. Everyone took off for their homes, like a prison break. The game ended instantly as visions of the police were strong for everyone involved. I ran home and acted like I was taking a nap. Patrick's sister kay Margaret was next door crying as she talked to my aunt Dorothy. Some of the guilty parties (mostly my cousins) were all present. My aunt went inside to call my uncle Lawrance at work.

Finally, my mom told me to get up and she walked me out to the court that was in session. We all looked guilty and did not try to exonerate ourselves. My mom told me, "Especially since you had never volunteered to take a nap before"! So, I joined my cohorts that were implicated in this alleged crime. My Aunt Dorothy started whipping her kids with a belt, and I had to suppress my laughter. Then my Uncle Lawrence arrived with vengeance for having to leave his job. He started whopping his kids in a way that would have gotten him arrested in today's world. I wasn't in a laughing mood anymore. I'm thinking to myself, will my mom let my uncle discipline me too? Then out of nowhere, my mom grabbed my arm and started whipping me with a belt. Then I was commanded to go and take a nap. I went directly into a deep sleep.

I became an entrepreneur at eight years old. I would cut grass with my step-grandfather's lawnmower. He charged me part of my profit for a usage fee. For using his lawn mower and for gas/oil. When he was not paying attention, my mom gave me the money right back. I had three customers and kept up with their lawns one day a week. I lost a really good a customer once because the Caesar boys (Timmy and Stef) bid my asking price. That lasted about three weeks until they were fired for poor work. Mr. Buddy contacted me to explain why he wanted me back. He said that I always raked up the cut grass and picked it up. He went on to tell me how when I cut his grass; it looked better than when Timmy and Stef did it.

Lastly, I got a raise as an incentive. When my step-grandfather asked how much I was getting for Mr. Buddy's yard, I told him. He started taking more out of my profits. There was nothing I could do about it...I essentially got penalized for my hard work.

I would later work for a friend of my birth mother. I started out just doing his yard. Then it turned into miscellaneous jobs. Fairly good money for that time period. I started out in my first endeavor as an entrepreneur, then as an employee. If I was older, I would have trained Timmy and Stef to work for me. Expanding my customer base for more profit. Incidentally, I started working at eight years old and am still at it at 62 years old.

CHAPTER 4

A SUMMARY OF MY EARLY YEARS

I discovered sports (Basketball, Football, and Baseball), and thank goodness for this. Sports was an effective way for me to get past the confusion in my life. It acted as an outlet to not dwell on the issues in my young beginnings and life. I played little league baseball for the Belair Braves. It ended up being the most rewarding sports experience of any other sport I participated in. The first season (only two seasons for ages 11th and 12th years old) wasn't so good. First, we got the worst-looking uniforms. While the other team, Mossville got great-looking uniforms. Ours fit like we were playing for a team from the 1920's. They were very baggy and ugly grey with green numbers and trim. We were basically beaten from start to finish. We didn't win a single ball game that season. Had to hear it all year long from the Mossville players. The next season was a totally different situation. For starters, we refused to wear those ugly uniforms. We decided to wear white T-Shirts and jeans. We won every game that season. I take immense pride in catching the last out in right field. One sad note, my birth mother never went to any of my baseball games ever!

Back when I was growing up, we had no television Until I was in grade school. I would go next door to my Aunt Dorothy's house to watch television. Before my Aunt Bernadine and my father Bob Ford left for New York, I would watch television at their house. I would go to the Ceasar's house sometimes and watch TV with Timmy and Stef. Not as much over there because of Kevin Caesar, another one of my bullies. We didn't get a colored TV until a couple of years before I joined the US Navy (In the the year 1979 while still in High School).

Louisiana summers are long and ridiculously hot, with suffocating humidity. Our house didn't have air conditioning, so we suffered. The house that had air conditioning was the Citizen's house. I knew this because I was always over there hanging out with my friend Patrick (also his brothers Larry and Chris, and his sister Donna Fe). I can't explain how hard it was to go to sleep at night in smothering heat. At our home, I had to kick one of my feet into the mattress, just to fall asleep.

At 3:15 pm the school bell rang to signify the end of the school day. We had five minutes to be through the pasture by 3:20 pm. If we were not through and out of the pasture, chances were great that we would have to fight. Older kids like Pump and Stan (and others) would be waiting for anyone trying to go through the pasture late. I got caught several times because of having to clean the chalkboard or the erasers (used on the chalkboards). The bigger kids would also catch us throughout the neighborhood. For any given time, for any unlucky kid who was not yet a teenager. I lost count of how many fights I was involved in. They made friends, fought friends, and had no mercy. You either fight another unlucky kid or get beat up by a big kid (teenager). Halloween was not safe either by any means. Since you had to "Trick or Treat" in a large group or not go. I got into one fight at recess, at school over my bald head. I knew how to fight by then because I had no choice. I had to have a bald head for a substantial portion of my childhood. I was once given the nickname "Baldy Bat." This nickname stuck with me in our neighborhood only and never made it to school. My mom would yell my nickname instead of my name when calling me to come home. It later changed to "Bally Bat." My uncle Alcede Jack the second, gave me this nickname. The son of my (enemy) Step grandfather, Alcede Jack the first.

I would go out and pick black berries for my mom all summer long.

Louisiana has 50 plus snakes, with at least 7 of them that are venomous. It was potentially dangerous to do something as simple as picking berries.

Would go fishing with remarkable success. Afterall, Louisiana is called "Sportsmen Paradise." I would catch crawfish and bull frogs because that is just what we Louisianians did. Many times, as we fished, snakes would come from nowhere and harass us. Sometimes we would leave for safety reasons, and other times we'd stay and take our chances.

We built what we called camps, which resembled wooden shacks. To me, they looked like makeshift buildings on the battle fields of the "Civil War." They were constructed of all sorts of scrap plywood, miscellaneous boards of all sizes, and two-by-fours. No one ever took a picture of these camps, but we were proud to "want to be carpenters."

One day out of the blue, my cousin Catherine (my Aunt Bernadine's oldest daughter) showed up with her two boys. Gabriel was around five or so, and Daniel was a newborn baby. They lived/stayed with us for a little while. They moved to Houston, Texas, and made it their home. I believe Catherine was waiting for my Aunt Bernadine to get set up in Houston first. Yes, my aunt had finally left my father (Bob Ford). My father would go on to marry Brenda and father my little sister and brother (Rason and Tesha).

Years later, Daniel would come and live with us for a whole school year (1st grade year). Then Daniel went back to Houston, Texas. He was adopted by Catherine's new husband Bonny Eason. For some reason, Gabriel was not adopted even though Gabriel and Daniel supposedly had the same father.

I spent several summers in Houston, Texas. We stayed at Catherine's house a lot and sometimes at Marie's house (Aunt Dorothy's oldest daughter). I would go on to spend several summers in Palmetto, Louisiana. I would stay with my great Aunt Tee fee (my mom's oldest sister). Palmetto is where my birth mother was born. My great grandmother MomYah (Ophelia Landrodeaux) was the midwife in my family, on my birth mother's side. During the Jim Crow era, Afro-Americans were not welcome in hospitals in the deep south. "New Orleans and Louisiana [are] the birthplace of separate but equal," said Alanah Odoms, the executive director of the ACLU of Louisiana, referring to the U.S. Supreme Court's decision in Plessy V. Ferguson, which made offering separate and racially segregated accommodations legal in the country. "If we're the birthplace of separate but equal then most of our institutions are going to reflect that history. In the same way that other institutions have been formed out of that history, the hospital and healthcare system would look the same." Quoted from the roots of New Orleans segregated hospitals started with a train ride, advocate says. By Josiah Bates October 6, 2023.

Many Afro American's just delivered their children at home by midwife. It is where most of my family was born prior to the mid to late fifties; was born at home by my great-grandmother MomYah. Louisiana was a dangerous place for Afro American's well into the 1960's and maybe a little beyond.

I joined the boy scouts as a ploy by my birth mother and this man named John "L." He was one of the men posing as my father (another Lie). He played the part by coming by and acting like he was my father. John "L" was a boy scouts troop leader, so I was placed in the boy scouts. I lost interest when my birth mother refused to buy any camping gear. Not even a uniform shirt was I allowed to get. The other kids (they had fathers) had all of the required gear and uniforms except me. My fake father never bought me anything… I wonder why? I later found out that Mr. John "L" had a whole family of his own. It was on to the next lie from this fiasco. I quit the Boy Scouts due to being humiliated. I stopped speaking to my birth mother for a while after that. Especially since she began telling me some other man was my father. She said this guy was dead. To get me to stop me from asking who my father was… I didn't stop!

I joined the Junior Deputies, which was a Sheriff's Department program for school-aged kids. I thrived in this discipline-style activity involving training. This gave me the first inkling of a possible military future. Other kids complained, but I took it as a challenge. I never was the complaining type. To me, it is what it is, just stay in the moment.

CHAPTER 5

THE JIM CROW YEARS

The Jim Crow laws were kept away from us kids by the grownups.

One effect of these laws was the segregation part. In my lifetime, I've experienced a portion of the Jim Crow laws. "Jim Crow laws were state and local laws introduced in southern states in the late 19th and early 20th centuries that enforced racial segregation, "Jim Crow being a pejorative term for an African American. Such laws remained in force until the mid-1960s." quoted from Wikipedia Jim Crow laws.

I went to an all-Afro-American school up to the 9th grade or 1976. This school was called Mossville Jr. High School. Opened in the year 1955 and permanently closed for good in 1991. In 1970, desegregation finally began for Mossville Jr. High students for 10th, 11th, and 12th graders would be going to other high schools. Westlake High and Sulphur High were the two schools, which was previously all Caucasian schools prior to this. The Mossville school would now be 1st through 9th grades. I started in Mossville in 1967 as a 1st grader. It obviously pre-seated desegregation, which put me directly as a person effected by "Jim Crow laws."

Jim Crow laws lasted into the 1970s in Louisiana. So, growing up in the 1960s and early 1970s had an effect on my peers and me directly. We stayed away from the city of Lake Charles, Westlake, and Sulphur Louisiana. Except for the occasional trip "Down East" to Palmetto, Louisiana (Where my birth mother's side of the family came from). I have never in my life seen the "Negro goes to the back door to order food "Signs" at restaurants. Neither have I ever seen Whites only water fountains (Negro only fountains as well). So-called Black parents kept all of the children away from any racism for our own protection. Racism and Jim Crow go hand in hand. I am so grateful they did this for us. I began attending Westlake high school in the fall of 1977. It was a shock to be around so many Caucasian kids. There was a major phenomenon that I witnessed at my new school. Probably more like a socially engineered phenomenon now that I think about it. Students split up according to race for some reason. All the Afro-Americans stayed in the front of the school during lunch breaks. In stark contrast, the

Caucasian American students stayed in the back of the school (Actually outside between the gym and the main building. desegregation at its finest and just as it was drawn up on all the plans.

CHAPTER 6

MY HALF-BROTHER AND SISTER

Paula is my half-sister as we share the same mother but different fathers. She moved into my mom's house after her death with our birth mother. Paula and I had a normal relationship. Some sibling rivalries, but nothing out of the ordinary. She had some tough times in her life, and I hurt for her to this day. I wish nothing but the absolute best for her. Paula has always been an avid reader of books, and very book smart in school at any level. She is a college graduate and has always been extremely locked in her studies. The fact that Billy, Paula, and I all have three different fathers (They always knew their fathers; I grew up not knowing). There has always been some degree of awkwardness between us three. I believe that we are commanded by the "Heavenly Father," to love thy neighbor. Therefore, how could I not love both of my half-siblings?

Once I was at one of Paula's events and she stood

up and talked about something that had happened to her in her youth. I was shocked to find out that my sister had been Raped twice by a cousin and an uncle.

Since I heard this on a hearsay basics, I cannot say their names. My rule is that if you don't have the exact facts about something...you really can't repeat what you have. Kinda like when the police must collect enough evidence to charge a suspect. I believed her story because it was so shockingly real.

My sister told our birth mother (Melba) each time that it happened, and she did nothing. It was the same recurring story in the deep south. We can't call the authorities because he is the sole breadwinner of his family. This is disgusting to me and wrong on many levels. Sadly, Paula and I don't talk

anymore for whatever reason.

Billy's father's last name (Alexander) was given to both Paula and I. Making Billy an actual Alexander. Paula is an actual Edwards, and I am an actual FORD!

Billy's Dad.... Joseph Alexander / Paula's Dad.... Hardy Edwards / Marvin's Dad.... Lester (Bob) Ford

My birth certificate had the wrong name for my father on it. The explanation from my birth mother was bizarre to me. She said that the hospital staff would not allow her to name me any other name that was different from her married name. Which was Alexander since she hadn't terminated her marriage with Joseph Alexander for a Decade (1951). She claimed to me that they made her use her married name, which was the name she was currently using at that time. She also claimed that Joseph Alexander was not there when all of this happened. Especially not when she gave birth to me. I find it hard to believe, but who knows? His signature is not on my birth certificate as my Father's. Only a typed-in name of his, so my birth mother could be telling the truth on this one thing.

Billy visited my Naval Base, which was nice of him. He loved me very much and I loved him. When my birth mother visited me in San Diego, California in 1983, it was a good visit. Billy had driven down from San Francisco, California to join us. I flew up to San Francisco several times to visit my big brother Billy. He really had a good bond with me. Once Billy came to a Naval Air Base (In Fallon, Nevada) where I was deployed for a few weeks. He picked me up and we went to Reno, Nevada for a really wonderful time. There was tasty food and some alcohol and girls involved in this deal. Leave it to Billy and just buckle up for a wild ride.

One memory of my half-brother Billy was the time he comforted me.

When my mom died, it was Billy and my sister Deborah who comforted me the most. I'll never forget that show of compassion. Billy died in 1994 of a heart attack. I immediately drove up to San Francisco. They would not release his body to me from the County Morgue. They would only release him to my birth mother (Melba). She refused to come to San Francisco for whatever reason. My uncle Herbert offered to pay for her flight, but still she said no! Because of this, my brother was cremated and buried in a mass grave.

CHAPTER 7

WHO AM I AND WHO IS SHE?

There was a time when I questioned my identity. This was when I was a young child. My birth mother just never made me feel secure in my understanding. In my young mind, all I could think of was who was I and who was she? She was vague on a plethora of questions that I asked her. I never got a straight answer most of the time, or I could not be sure. So confusing was this period for me.

My birth mother started being untruthful about who my father was around the time I was nine years old. I really wanted to know who my father was…very badly. I suffered mentally and physically and who knows what else. It was tough when most (or all) of my neighborhood knew of my predicament. I would stare into a mirror for lengthy periods of time.

Wondering who I was and where I came from. I even thought that I might have been Kidnapped at birth. I have never contemplated suicide at any time in my life. My birth mother had me so messed up with all the lies and deception. It became so confusing and made it hard to know what was reality or deception.

Grown-ups were unfriendly or even mean to me. I was a quiet kid and not a troublemaker at all. The only thing that comes to mind for me is probably the adulterous act done by my birth mother. How she got pregnant with me. Secondly, many people knew what had happened between my birth mother and my father. I guess I was blamed for it, merely for existing. My birth mother never protected me. But my mom did protect me all the way up to her death. After her death, I was fair game for manipulation.

I started doubting if Melba was my real mother, as I became more confused. But if my mom said she was, the case would be closed. She did just that so it's official in my mind. My mom did not lie. The funny thing is that I never asked my mom who my father was. My grandmother: Mom, was my rock always. I just don't understand the Lying about who my father was.

One day my birth mother admitted to me who my father was, by name (Bob Ford). A few days later, she went back to denying it all, vehemently! Finishing with, I didn't need a dad. Also, saying that Paula didn't have a dad either. I thought she was losing her mind. Then I realized what happened. She was put back in line by those in the family who wanted this kept a secret.

The abortion subject came up when I was already an adult. It still hurts to know that your birth mother even considered aborting me. Even though abortion was not legal in 1961, there were ways to get it done. My birth mother said that if she had the money, I would have been aborted. It was a huge scandal about how my birth mother got pregnant with me. I feel lucky to be here and am a supporter of Life (pro-life). I'm pro-life to the moon and back.

CHAPTER 8
MY REAL MOM AND BIRTH MOTHER

My real mom (grandmother) and mother of my birth mother's name was Evelyn King Jack. My birth mother's name is Melba King Anderson. They were nothing alike, not even close. My birth mother was the woman who gave birth to me, and I am grateful for that. I have had indignation toward her many times. But I have never hated her. The birth father issues have been extremely frustrating. Maybe even rising to a form of child abuse, in my opinion. Once my birth mother brought me some shoes to wear to school. They were women's shoes and white in color. I later found out that they were shoes for a female nurse. I got teased at school, which was not easy to deal with. My birth mother thought this was funny for some odd reason. There were good things that my birth mother did too. For instance, the ten-year-old birthday gift I received from her (a wristwatch). I loved that watch so much.

Every Easter, I'd get a cowboy hat filled with candy and small toys. She got me an electric train set. I loved this train set so much. It was my favorite gift of my entire childhood. My step-grandfather would eventually burn it in a fire destroying it forever. It took a long time to get over that trauma. I looked forward to every gift every year. My birthdays came and went without much of a celebration when I was growing up. To this day, I really don't make a big deal about it at all. My birth mother kept the identity of my father a secret for all my childhood years. If she had told me the truth, I would have protected her. It undoubtedly would have angered many in the family. The secret of Marvin's birth father's identity was to remain one. I wasn't aware of any hostilities directed toward my birth mother. But maybe a couple of people, like my aunt Dorothy and my step-grandfather Alicede Jack the first. They hated her just as they hated me. Because of this, I felt compelled to take up for her (a Louisianan way of explaining protecting someone). My birth mother's enemies were also mine. Overall, my relationship with my birth mother has been rocky for years. With that being said, I follow what the laws and commandments of Yahuah (God) command us to do.

One of these commandments is to honor thy mother and father. I forgave my birth mother (Melba) a long time ago. I honor her with respect and gratitude for allowing me to be here on this earth. I speak to my birth mother by telephone as often as I can. We discuss anything she wishes. I never bring up anything pertaining to my birth father. Enough pain has come over everyone concerned. We basically have a bible study in many of our calls. I am amazed at her zest for life and seemingly no stress. I don't want to hurt her in any way, especially things from the past. We talked a lot about Mom, as we rekindled all the beautiful memories.

While attending my brother Larry's funeral, I found out from my cousin that my uncle Alicede Jack II mentioned something important. Uncle Jack admitted who my father was, while my cousins Sherrell and Deborah were present. Uncle Jack did it by accident and regretted it instantly (deep family secret). The cat is out of the hat, but the deception is still going strong. I mentioned this to my birth mother on a phone call. Her reply was sharply toned, "He knows more than me." I dropped it right there with a sardonic look on my face. No need to stress her out, as she continues to keep the deep family secret suppressed (or so she thinks). The secret is no longer and is widely known. I pray that my birth mother does repent and asks for forgiveness. I want her to go to heaven. She is nearly 90 years of age and still going strong. I ask everyone who reads my Memoir, to also pray for my birth mother (Melba Theresa King Anderson). The past cannot be changed. I say let's all just live in the present.

My mom, my birth mother's mother was my savior. She was the smartest person I have ever known. Yes, even without ever going to school. Born in August of the year 1908, in the state of Louisiana. Also, to Ophelia, known to everyone as "MomYah." A Hebrew name, but she spoke only French Creole. MomYah was born in the year 1877. How ironic for my great-grandmother MomYah and my Paternal grandfather Joseph Ford to speak Hebrew are be called a Hebrew name. Mom (Evelyn King-Jack) was a very tenacious person, who had to improvise her way through life. Her patience with having to raise me was unbelievable. Especially being an older person when I was dropped off at her home. As if I was an orphan without a home. I'm so grateful that my mom taught me valuable life lessons.

Punishment and rewards were given with an equal amount of love. I got what they called Louisiana, a whipping. Whippings in the form of corporal punishment. The reason why I feel Mom did this is an act of love. Is because she kept a running tally of all my wrongdoings. After enough of them were accumulated, she would go over each of them (a learning moment). After this, then it was the decisive moment...punishment. It was just the way things happened during that period of my life. We also got reprimanded at school, with a paddle. Usually, a wooden paddle would hurt badly. Neighbors got in on the whipping as well. Once I threw a rock and accidentally hit a parked car. I got a whipping from that neighbor after he called my mom. My mom gave this neighbor permission to whip me with a switch (a small limb cut from a branch of a tree), which was most effective when it was still green. This switch from a tree branch that was not rotten. Trust me when I say that these switches were very painful and got the point across. Once the neighbor was done whipping me, I was sent home. Once home, I came to realize that my list of infractions had accumulated to a higher amount on the punishment list.

I found out once, that not being upfront (truthful) or omitting information was the same as lying. (example) There I was goofing off with a classmate in our third-grade classroom. Plucking a Nickle, hockey-style on my desktop. For some unknown reason, I decided to put the Nickle in my mouth. I inadvertently swallowed the Nickle, to the surprise of Wyman Thibodaux (my classmate). My first mistake was not telling my teacher (Mrs. Young). Wyman told the teacher (without my knowledge) instead of me...not good. My second mistake was not telling my mom when I got home from school. Low and behold to my complete astonishment, Mrs. Young, my 3rd grade teacher knocked on our front door. When I saw her, I had no idea that my classmate Wyman had told her about my swallowing the Nickle. My mom and Mrs. Young sat down with coffee and discussed what happened. I found out that I had lied by not telling them both. I was informed that my punishment list had increased. When Mrs. Young left, I was given castor oil, to pass the Nickle out as I defecated. My cousin (from next door) Calvin fished it out of my stool...YUCK! He actually kept it for heaven's sake. There was no lying allowed in our home... period. I feel blessed for the the many biblical teachings I learned from my mom.

Once, I set a house fire underneath my mom's bed. There were people visiting with my mom in our living room. I was in my mom's bedroom trying to look under her bed for a toy. For some unknown reason, I decided to set fire to a sheet of rolled-up paper. Lighting it in the gas-open flame heater. This heater was open with access to the flames. I put this flame-lit paper under her bed. Of course, it caught fire, and I ran to the living room where everyone else was. Oh, I had even closed the door to the bedroom. I sat down and didn't tell anyone what I had done. I must have had a guilty look on my face because my mom kept staring at me (she knew something was up). Finally, my uncle Lawrance smelled the smoke and ran into the bedroom. They were able to put the fire out quickly. I felt so guilty and ashamed of myself for letting my mom down, by not saying what happened. My mom never gave me a whipping for this. The look that she gave me made me desire a whipping. It turned out to be the ultimate lesson on lying. Thinking back on this event, it was like my mom used psychology in this situation. I was a good kid for a very long time after that incident.

When my mom died, I didn't know how to understand it. I really did not believe it until I saw her in the casket. As I sat with my sister Deborah at her funeral, I was numb. My sister was crying and wanted to know why I was not crying as well. I did not know why but was comforted by her sitting with me. I miss my mom's wisdom and her positive vibe. She saved me from my birth mother. I don't even know how I would have turned out without her in my life. I do wonder what my mom would have said if I had asked her who was my father. She would not have lied. Too much moral clarity in her for that. I do miss her a lot, even to this very day. I will be visiting my mom's grave soon.

Gladys Knight's Lyrics
For her song:
"You're the best thing that ever happened to me."
<u>I dedicate this song to my mom.</u>
<u>Evelyn King Jack</u>
<u>RIP</u>

I've had my share.
Of life's ups and downs.
But fate's been kind. The downs have been few.
I guess you could say.
I've been lucky.
Well, I guess you could say that it's all because of you.
If anyone.
Should ever write.
My life story.
For whatever reason there might be

Ooh, you'll be there between each line of pain and
glory. 'Cause you're the best thing that ever happened
to me.
(You're the best thing that ever happened to me) Ah,
you're the best thing that ever happened to me.
…Oh, there have been times when times were hard.
But always somehow, I made it, I made it through.
'Cause for every moment that I've spent hurting.
There was a moment that I spent, ah, just loving you.
…I anyone should ever write my life story.
For whatever reason there might be.
Oh, you'll be there between each line of pain and glory.
'Cause you're the best thing best thing that ever
happened to me.
(You're the best thing that ever happened to me).
…Oh, you're the best thing that ever happened to me.
**That never happened to me: (You're the best thing,
oh that ever happened to me).**
I know, you're the best thing, oh, that ever happened
to me.

She was the best thing to happen to me. I owe her
everything, but there is no way to show my gratitude. I
love her with all of my heart and yes, I still remember
that "The truth shall set you free." My mom kept my
life stable in a home with structure. She was not easy
on me but instead raised me to become the Alpha male
that I am today. Yes, it is true that my life seemed to be
like a "house of cards" because of my confusing birth

mother's deception. My mom gave me the strength to allow those cards to fall where they may. I look back now and marvel at my mom's ability to basically be a mother and a father to me. I have a keen ability to have patience and a keen sense of Virtue. She taught me how to read people as well as the temperature in a room (meaning different personalities). She was my Rock and in a roundabout way, my force within myself. Especially after her death, which I still mourn to this very day.

CHAPTER 9

THE FUSELIER'S, MY NEXT-DOOR COUSIN'S

My cousins who lived next door to my mom and me, were very much in my life's story. Darrell and I were only six months apart in age.

Darrell was the quiet type and not confrontational. He and I played together a lot growing up. We just fell out of touch in our adult years. I took off for the US Navy to escape my confusing life. Really never returned to make Louisiana my home. It was inevitable as I got away from my father's issues.

Lawrence Jr. was like ten years older than I was. We didn't have many interactions, but when we did it was positive. He was always nice to me. I liked him as being just a nice guy. I wish him well in whatever he is doing nowadays.

Fredrick, who everyone just called Glen, was younger than I. The only problem I ever had with Glen was when we were adults. I was between enlistments in the Navy, and spending time in Louisiana for a year. Stef, Glen, and I were playing street basketball one day. Glen became overly aggressive toward me. At one point, he started saying how he wanted to punch me. Keep in mind this wasn't new to me, in other situations in my native Louisiana. I grew up having to fight since everyone knew that I had no father around. Not to provoke him, I stayed calm in a calculated ready for whatever mode. In other words, being calm does not mean I wasn't ready to defend myself. I don't know this for certain, but I think he sensed my readiness. He backed off and tried to laugh it off. I stayed on the ready. We were never the same after that incident. I'll never trust Glen again, after that. His Wife died not too many years ago. I called him to give my condolences, but he didn't answer. I left a message, but he never replied. I'm okay with that, especially since he was in mourning.

Calvin was always nice to me. He was older than I, but we hung out from time to time. On several occasions, he and I would make homemade French fries and fried pork chops. I wish him well, and best wishes.

Unfortunately, Calvin and I have no relationship at all.

Barbra Jean is my absolute favorite of them all. She helped me with homework and was genuinely nice to me always. I loved sitting down and listening to Barbra and my mom discussing bible verses. I can't remember how many times she has taught me something new. I would watch Barbra dance when "Soul Train" was on television. She had an impressive skill of both singing and dancing. To this day, Barbra is my favorite Fuselier.

Marie, the oldest child of Dorothy, my aunt. Marie always made me feel welcome. I would go to her house and play with her kids (James, Rita, and Otis). She let Patrick and I stay at her home in Houston once. With no problems at all. Made us feel right at home. I have not seen her since my brother Freddy's funeral. As a kid, I spent some summers in Marie's home and those were some great memories. She will always be dear to my heart.

Michael and I had problems growing up. He was three years older than I was. Michael beat me up every now and then. It really wasn't that big of a deal. Boys will be boys, and we were always challenging each other. Of course, he was bigger and stronger than I, with the age difference. But I never backed down, which was a bad idea most of the time. One of my key issues with Michael was his friend Kevin Ceasar. Who was the brother of Tim and Stef? Kevin would bully me, and Michael would do nothing about his behavior. At this time, I hated Michael for not standing up for me. We would play very physical basketball games. I would get hurt by Michael and run to tell my aunt Dorothy. As usual, she would do nothing about it. I came to my senses and stopped going to her to complain. This made my relationship with Michael worse. I was on my own, with no father to counsel me in any way. It was a stressful time especially since it was them against me. Kevin was riding a horse one day. He has seen me walking down the street. For no good reason, he decided to scare me. So, he rode the horse right up to me. I was not scared at all. All I could think of was how to get even with this guy. His mother, Mrs. Ceasar yelled at him to stop. Then he let me pass, I gave him a look that could kill. After a big rainstorm one day, I was walking home when I encountered Michael and his best friend Kevin. At the corner of 6th Street and Michigan Avenue near the ditches, which was full of water from the earlier rainstorm.

As I walked by them, Kevin started grabbing and pushing me toward the l ditch (full of water). I yelled at Michael to help me. Michael did nothing but laugh. Kevin was bigger than I, so he eventually was able to push me into the ditch. I was angrier at my cousin Michael than Kevin. I hated my cousin and told him just that. They both laughed at me, but finally allowed me to exit the ditch. I was humiliated and full of rage. I did not talk to my cousin for weeks after that. I wanted to fight Kevin; a no-win scenario that I knew. It would have given me pleasure to hurt him in any way. I have had no communication with Kevin for decades now. I am now 6' 7" and 235 pounds with an athletic build, so I'd just leave it with that thought. Michael and I made it past all of that. Michael also introduced professional sports and football players to me on TV and I am forever thankful to him for that. There are residual effects from being bullied all those years of growing up. Those effects are the realization of how it all made me stronger. So, thank you to all my bullies from yesteryear.

CHAPTER 10
MY MOM MARRIES MY ENEMY.

My mom married my enemy when I was 8 years old. He was the father of my mom's two youngest sons. Who bears the same last name as "Jack." Her sons Alicede Jack II and Herbert Jack were my uncles. My mom's new husband, Alicede Jack would become my enemy. Apparently, Alicede Jack I, which I'll refer to as my step-grandfather, hated me. I found out decades later why. It was because of the way my birth mother got pregnant with me. He also hated my birth mother as well. I don't think he ever confronted my birth father, ever. He took it out on me since my birth mother stood up to him. I was not able to do that and was stuck there with him. It was a tough few years for me. Up until my mom passed away. My step-grandfather moved out to avoid living with my birth mother. Who moved in immediately upon my mom's death. I will now explain what I meant by my step-grandfather being my enemy.

While standing next to my step-grandfather, as he talked to my mom.

Who was standing on the backdoor steps? At some point, she must have been calling my name. I was daydreaming and off into LaLa land. So, I did not hear her at first. Finally, I was jolted out of my daydream, and I yelled out loudly, "What"! My step-grandfather slapped me so hard; that I woke up or came to lying flat on my back. Then I looked up just in time to hear my mom speak. She told him, "If you ever hit Marvin again like that, I'll kill you"!

He never hit me like that again, but he still used his belt on me.

After getting home from school in the afternoon. I started watching my favorite TV show, "Lost in Space." My cousin Darrell kept coming inside to tell me that my step-grandfather wanted me outside. Back in those days, once you missed a TV program, which was it. No recordings or savings on a DVR to watch later. I was hooked on this show big time. I finally went outside (after the show was over) and he was waiting for me. He was truly angry at me. Which scared me to the core. I thought he was going to kill me. I had not yet seen him that angry before. My cousin Darrell standing at the 9 o'clock position, my step-grandfather at the 12 o'clock position with I standing at the 6 o'clock position facing him straight on.

Darrell started to laugh in anticipation of my demise. When I saw him laughing, I made up my mind that I would not let him hit me. Suddenly, my step-grandfather started removing his belt. Darrell laughed even harder, which made my indignation toward him grow even stronger. Then came the decisive moment! He got his belt out and swung it at my head. I timed it perfectly and ducked under the rapidly approaching belt. I looked up just in time to see the belt connected with Darrell's face. A thick swollen welt rose up on his face. This distracted my enemy just long enough for my escape. I sprung up and ran to the only hiding place my step-grandfather could not get me. Under the house and safe from capture. When I got there, I cried and then I laughed. The worst thing was that I knew he would get me later. That evening, I was placed under a chair with my buttocks exposed. I hurt for many days after this beating. My only consolation was the fact that Darrell had gotten what he deserved. I was not allowed to see another "Lost in Space" TV show until my enemy left for good.

I had a playhouse, which I built myself. All of us kids called them a camp. One of the things we used to play in these camps was war games (Simulated only). We would play in our camps for hours. There were harmless raggedy-looking buildings, which was a lot of fun. On one particular day, I came home from school and my camp was gone. My step-grandfather decided it needed to be destroyed. He told me why, but I only saw his mouth moving, but no sound came out. I genuinely believed that I was in some form of shock. I could not understand it or why. I wished to die or just leave forever. He was now a true enemy of mine.

My birth mother gave me an electric train set one Christmas. It was the single greatest gift I had ever gotten. I really loved my train set, and my step-grandfather knew it. He also knew that it was given to me by my birth mother. He Hated me being happy. Sometime later, he told me to get rid of my train set (out of nowhere). I cried at the realization of possibly having my train set taken away. Then I decided I would not throw away my beloved train set. I hid it under the house in my hiding place. That only worked for an abbreviated time, unfortunately. My step-grandfather got my cousin Glen to climb under our house and do his dirty work. Glen retrieved my train set and my step-grandfather burned it up in a fire. What a coincidence, he timed it perfectly. As I was just arriving from school, is when the flames were at their strongest. I prayed for my father (whoever he was) to come and get me. I wanted to run away, but to where? I was only 8 years old with zero chance of escaping my tormentor.

I got a dog from a neighbor and really enjoy him a lot. The dog was like a therapy dog for me. Something I really needed, dealing with my enemy daily. As I got happier with my dog, it must have infuriated my step-grandfather. One day I was told by him that I had to get rid of my dog. How was I to do that, and why? He tormented me for a week or two, about my dog. Then the day I now call, "Armageddon." He called me outside, not having any idea what he wanted. When I located him, he was in a wooded area beside our home. He had my dog tied up to a tree. He had that really frightening look of anger on his face. My heart almost stopped beating at this point. Then I instantly got scared and extremely nervous. He scolded me for not getting rid of my dog. I said nothing because I was frozen in place and couldn't move. I was confused about exactly what was happening. I was thinking maybe I should run. Will he kill me or just hit me with the shovel? So, without warning, he picked up the shovel and killed my dog right in front of me. If I was not in shock before, I was now. He then threw the shovel at me and angrily yelled out, "Bury It"! As he stomped off in the direction of the house. I was only 8 or 9 years old. I thought he would kill me too. In a sickening way, I was a little relieved when he threw the shovel at me. It meant I wasn't next to be killed. I don't remember burying my dog. I was too numb and in shock.

My step-grandfather would embarrass me in front of my friends. Like, force me to empty a Pot when I had a friend over. I would always hide the Pot's and pray that my friends visiting, did not have to defecate. We could urinate outside, if necessary.

Once, we found a dead pig down the road, and all of us decided to drag it home. Leave it to boys to do stupid things. Of course, this was to impress my step-grandfather. It was a decision made by all of us. I was one of the youngest in the group (which is important to mention). When we got home with this dead pig, I was attacked by my enemy. He blamed the whole thing directly on me. He made me feel as low as possible. This man raged me out for what seemed like hours, in front of the other kids. I was affected by it, but confused about why no one spoke up on my behalf. They let me get torn down, knowing it was not true. My step-grandfather treated my cousins very well. My treatment of him was the opposite. I had no idea what to do about my predicament. My mom had little control since he was the head of the household.

My step-grandfather belittled me every chance he got. He would order me around military style. You see, he served in World War I, in the US Army. He was mean to me. He hated me, which at the time I was clueless about the reason why. However, there is one unseen benefit. He did get me hooked on Baseball. When we watched Baseball on TV, I was safe from his hate. Overall, I dreaded living with him period. When my step-grandfather died, I was ten years old. At his funeral, I showed nothing. I had a blank face and I never cried. He was my nemesis and any other menacing description I can think of.

CHAPTER II

THE LITTLE FARM AND SO MUCH MORE

I basically grew up on a tiny little farm. I think the only thing my mom got from the grocery was Milk, dairy, and miscellaneous product items. The milkman came around and delivered milk. We had chickens, Pigs, and a good-sized garden. I had fun here plus the food was organic and fresh. My uncle Lawrence (who was married to my aunt Dorothy) would share his hunting kills sometimes. Rabbits, squirrels, raccoons, armadillos, fresh fish, and crabs. There was plenty of food around as we mainly eat from the land, and less from the grocery stores.

My jobs were many, but I did not mind it at all. I loved helping out since it gave me a good feeling. I would slop (feed) the hogs every day as one of my chores. It was a hard job, but it felt good to complete this and other task. Feeding the chickens was one of the easiest chores. The picking of chicken eggs was a lot more challenging to accomplish. Mainly because of this mean Red Rooster, we had. This Rooster would chase me all the time. I was not scared, but I was overly cautious of this crazy Rooster. He attacked Darrell once, causing him to have to be rescued by one of the adults. I must admit that I did laugh because it was funny. I told him not to stop running, but he stopped anyway. Another chore I had was to go get water every day. At my Aunt Bernadine's and Uncle Bob's (my father). That gave me time to play with Larry, Freddy, and Deborah. My actual siblings at the time were unbeknownst to me. I knew them only as my cousins. Then came the hideous chore of emptying out the pots from their various locations in the house. The yard work was a big one, though not my favorite. I did get particularly good at it. Plus, it gave me some level of pride to see how well our yard always looked. All these chores gave me a splendid work ethic. This was beneficial for my ability to complete future tasks. And having pride in being responsible in doing a task correctly. I started washing dishes at an early age. I became particularly good at it, which gave me pride in pleasing my mom by being good at it. It was a rather tedious chore, and I did not love it. On the other hand, it helped develop me to be more patient.

There was no garbage collection in our neighborhood. Everyone had to burn their trash. Some used a 5-gallon barrel, and some just either burned the trash on the ground or dug a hole. I did not burn trash, since it was a job for an adult to do. One day, Darrell, Fredrick (Glen), Paula, and I were standing around watching the trash fire. I was kneeling on the ground playing in the fire. When suddenly, I got pushed from behind. I landed on my hands first in the fire. Burning both of my hands, with the right hand being burned the worst. I started screaming, as the pain became unbearable. I had no idea who had pushed me in, but I knew it was not an accident. I was pushed hard. It turns out to be Paula who was allegedly the guilty one. Both Darrell and Fredrick pointed at her as the one who had pushed me. She denied it, but still got a whipping from one of the adults (Aunt Florance I think). I wasn't my mom, because she was tending to my injuries. I had at least a second-degree burns on both hands. There were blisters on both tops of my hands. But again, the worst of it was on my right hand. No doctor, just my incredible mom as my honorary Physician took care of me. In hindsight, I really don't know who pushed me into the fire, so I cannot give an opinion. I did get a new respect for fire after this experience.

Every Saturday, we did the house cleaning. It was an all-hands effort. We dusted and cleaned from top to bottom. Swept the floors from the front to the back of the house. My mom had so many superstitions (a Louisiana thing). I couldn't keep up with all of them. For instance, we had to be careful while sweeping. If the broom hit your feet, you had to spit on it so that you would not go to jail. I still do this one to this very day. My wife just shakes her head at me when she witnesses this. Another one was never swept out of the front door. If you did, you would sweep someone out of the house. Once the sweeping was done, it was time to mop the house. All the floors were thoroughly moped, which bought out the true beauty of the solid wood floors. I would watch my mom make soup from scratch. Which made the house smell so delicious, a fond memory I'll always keep.

The Lye soap that she made in a large pot over a wood fire outdoors.

This soap was used for washing our clothes. I was so impressed with my mom, a real do-it-all type. She would explain things to me at a level that I could understand. An extraordinary woman who was a joy to just watch her work.

My mom would slaughter chickens with ease. She either broke their necks with just a few twists. Grabbing the chicken's neck and with a circular motion until the neck broke. Death was almost instantaneous. The other way took some getting used to, for me as an onlooker. The chicken was basically beheaded with an Ax.

When they butchered a hog, I was told to stay back and just watch.

There was nothing for a kid to do but watch. My uncle Lawrence would shoot the hog in the forehead. It would immediately die, which amazed me with pure astonishment. My mom would then cut the throat with a knife to collect the blood for sausages (Yuck)! Then they would have a fifty-five-gallon barrel heated up with water over a fire. The next step would be to dump the dead hog into the very hot water. After that process was finished, they would remove all the hair. Which was the reason for the hot water. I would lose interest after this stage of the butchering process. I'd go play with my cousins or my friend Patrick. The actual cutting up of the animal was not my cup of tea.

CHAPTER 12
MY MOM DIED.

When my mom died, I was lost without her. She was my security and protector. When I think of her, what comes to mind is mountains shoring up into the clouds. A larger-than-life hero that I would never get to at least say goodbye to. I knew she was sick, but not that sick. It was so weird to see her leave home for the hospital. I was left home alone with my enemy (step-grandfather). He must have been worried about Mom like I was. I did not get clobbered once in her absence. It was a hot August early evening with the sun still out. My step-grandfather and I were sitting on the porch.

Remember, there were no cell phones or social media in 1971. Suddenly, my Aunt Dorothy's car approached their driveway. As the car doors started opening, it was obvious something was wrong. Aunt Dorothy, my birth mother, and my cousin Barbra all got out of the car. Everyone was crying hard. I froze where I was sitting. I think my step-grandfather asked them what was wrong. One of them, I don't remember who said that my mom had passed away in the hospital. I remember wondering just what that meant. Shortly after this, my birth mother told me that my mom was dead. She said that Mom was not coming back. I was shocked, confused, and scared when this was confirmed.

My birth mother moved in almost immediately. Then the arguments started. Melba and Alicede did not like each other. I did not care about them and their war of words, back and forth. All I knew was that my mom was never coming back. Eventually, my step-grandfather moved out to live with his son (my uncle) Alicede Jack II. It was a pleasant feeling to see him go. There were no goodbyes or any words between him and me. The next time I saw him, it was at his funeral. And we never spoke again. He would die a few years later. I was forced to attend my enemy's funeral because otherwise, I would not have gone. He was out of my life, but the scares remained. He made my personality stronger and made me a tougher-minded person.

There were many ways in which my mom enriched my life. Still, to this very day, I use principles taught to me by her. My Moral aptitude has been set since I was a kid. She was the most honest person I have ever known. And I try and emulate her every day of my life. I will hold her high on a pedestal because she is worthy of it in my opinion. To my knowledge, I have never seen anyone angry with my mom. Just as I have never seen her angry with anyone either.

My mom taught me so much about life. Like how to prepare myself before leaving home. Brush my teeth and wash my face. Didn't have to worry about hair, because I had none. Once a week I had to go down to Mr. Thibodaux's barber shop. Where I got all my hair cut off (to the scalp). I called it "an Ivoly (pronounced I-vo-ly) V-3." I made it up to avoid the term Bald head, which I hated. This tied into my nickname, "Bally Bat." Head like a baseball and body like a baseball bat.

Mom taught me to have a strong work ethic. I developed into a very patient worker. I was known for always getting the job done. Then talk about the issues or problems after the job is completed. Never any excuses, which would have meant that the job didn't get finished. She taught me to blame only myself when something went wrong. To challenge myself instead of blaming others when I fail. How to properly shake someone's hand. Keeping eye contact while shaking hands. When speaking to someone, I was to always look them in the eyes. If the other person did not look me in the eye, they didn't respect me. I had forgotten some of the ethical techniques taught to me by my mom. But was reintroduced to them through life experiences.

She taught me how to be a good Christian. I learned how to say the lord's prayer. From a gentle and compassionate style of teaching by my mom. I noticed that she read the bible often. The tenth commandments were observed and practiced in our home daily. Lying was forbidden and not tolerated. I just didn't lie to my mom or anyone else. I went to Sunday school every single Sunday morning. No matter what the weather was like. I was also at every Sunday church service. Twice on First Sunday for communion. I am a very patient person today because of my mom. All the religious activities helped me to be very humble. Understanding what my mom went through to raise me is mind-boggling to me now. She took on the responsibility of raising me seriously.

I grew up at a time when children were quiet around adults. My mom taught me how to listen first and speak last. Everyone may have heard the saying, "The smartest person in the room is the quietest person in the room." The adults would not ask children what they liked when preparing their food. We had to remain quiet and accept whatever they put on our plates. Oh, and we were expected to eat it all, or else. It was stressful to deal with it, but what else could we do (nothing)? If a kid mistakenly spoke during an adult conversation, he or she would be in danger of being punished. They might just reprimand the kid with a warning. Consider yourself lucky with a warning, trust me on that. The adult might say to the guilty kid, "Stay out of grown folk conversations"! We were all taught to respect our elders. So, there were no excuses. I was also taught to be courteous, (Southern Style). Meaning, it was yes/no Ma'am; yes/no Sir. Mr. / Mrs. and expected.

I never asked my mom who my father was. I thought why should I ask my mom? It was on Melba to come clean. Whatever the reason for my birth mother lying to me, was between us. I knew that my mom had nothing to do with the mess of my existence. I never asked my Aunt Bernadine either, for the same reason. She was the injured party in this thing too. It was her husband (my uncle/father) that got with my birth mother and made me. The onus is on my birth mother and no one else. I still have pain from losing my mom. I have so much love for her. RIP, Mom!

CHAPTER 13

MY BIRTH MOTHER MOVES IN

My birth mother moved in after my mom died. It was fireworks between Melba and Alcide Jack I. They argued about anything and everything.

Melba would yell out, this is in my momma's house. Alcide would yell back, she was my wife. He would proudly tell Melba how Mom had two children with him. Uncle Alcide Jack II and Uncle Herbert Jack to which my step-grandfather was referring. They argued morning noon and night. I was glad not to be in danger of any more abuse from him. My birth mother protected me by her mere presence. Yes, my mom let things go on. She was from a period where men ruled over women. Sort of like being submissive to their husbands. Her place was below my step-grandfather, like in the olden days. He was born in the late 1800s and my mom was right behind him in 1908. To protect my mom, I never told her anything that he had done to me. First, because of what he might do to her. Secondly, I remembered what she told him if he ever hit like that again. When he slapped me hard one time, my mom said that she would kill him if he did that again. Anyway, my step-grandfather moved out, finally. I was a happy little boy after this happened.

No more bald heads for me. Melba tried to indicate they should continue. In the end, I won, and finally, I could grow an Afro. It was bell-bottom pants and large collared shirts once Melba showed up. I became more independent. I also became more frustrated about why she kept giving false names of guys being my father. Eventually, it became apparent that all she was doing was lying to me. I asked her often who my father was. Finally, I got more withdrawn with more anger setting in. I never attempted suicide, but I thought about it. I daydreamed about how it would be if I wasn't around. In almost every dream, I was not missed at all. At some point, which thought of killing myself went away. I never went back there again. Sometimes I used to wonder just how far I might have gone through with such a heinous act. I would visit this suicide thing later in life. Losing my daughter to it when she was only 16 years old.

We seem to get poorer after Melba moved in. Less food was available in our home. The once thriving little farm was no more. About this time, I was introduced to grocery stores for the first time. My first time eating at McDonald's was when I was in high school. In the grocery store for the first time. I had never seen so much food in one place. I quickly lost interest in going after a while though. Melba wouldn't let me pick anything. I stopped going and just ate whatever she purchased. I don't blame her because money was very tight for us.

I started spending a lot of time at the Citizen's house. My best friend Patrick's family. When I first went to his house, Paula came too. Both Paula and I were amazed at how much difference there was between their home and our home. It was the first colored Television I had ever seen. They had air conditioning, which was another first. Patrick had sisters and brothers, but the most important thing was his two parents. They had something I had never seen, a family structure. They all treated me like one of their own. In my mind, they are family to me. When I came home after Navy Boot Camp, I went straight to see Mrs. Citizen. I loved Patrick's mom and dad to the moon and back. I learned a lot from that household, which carried me through life. I am grateful to all the Citizen family for the love and the family experience.

I got disgusted with the lies about who my father was. The older I got the angrier I became. Not much I could do at my youthful age. I knew deep down, I had to get away from Melba and all the lies. One day she tells me that my father is a Preacher. I was very skeptical about allowing myself to believe any of that. After I hit her with a barrage of questions, it went nowhere.

Obviously, it was just another lie. Now we were right back where we started. The next time we get to another discussion about my father's identity. Melba tells me that my father is married to someone else with a family. What am I supposed to do with this? Someone with a family, really! I asked the usual questions. It all ended up right where it always ends up, nowhere. I started begging Melba to tell me who my father might be. She would brush me off, or simply refuse to answer. The next go around was her informing me that my father was dead. This was an effort to end my curiosity for good. To Melba's amazement, I went on to question her like a lawyer would. I knew she did not like it, and even showed some anger. I didn't care since I too was angry. All the while when I'm trying to find out about my father. He is in New York, married with children. He died when I was about to get out of the US Navy. She purposely kept me from ever having any type of relationship with him. I would ask her for his name. I wanted to know my Identity. Which I feel would have made a major difference in my life. So, I continued to push for the truth about my father's Identity. The anger and withdrawn feelings continued. Thank goodness for sports! Then one day she tries to pull off an illusion. She went from your father is dead, to no he is not dead. She admitted lying about my father's death. Then pivoted to yet another man as my father. Except for the first time, this one had a name. I was also going to meet this man. Mr. Williams shows up at our house as my new dad. He played the part for a few months until he got tired of it, is my guess. Later, Mr. Williams started hanging around more. Spending more time with me. I started believing this to be true. Mr. Williams introduces me to the Boy Scouts. Where he was a scout leader. He would take me to church and sit with me sometimes. I thought this man was my real father, falling for it 100%. But nope, it was just another lie. This manipulation by Melba conspiring with dear old fake dad (Mr. Williams). After the gig was over, everything went back to normal confusion for me. Mr. Williams stops coming by and ignores me everywhere I see him in public. Melba finally admits that it was all a lie.

Treats it as if she did it for my own good. After I, of course, demanded an explanation then she caved. To be said, Mr. Williams was not my father. It hurt me deeply until I couldn't even look at Melba for some time afterward. Thank goodness for my best friend's family, "The Citizens."

I felt empty all through high school. The only reason I made it through was because I played sports. I played football for one reason really.

Because of the physical aspect of this sport. My grades suffered all throughout high school. Not because I was not smart enough. It was all the issues pertaining to my existence. The deep family secret, concerning me. A secret that I had no understanding about at the time. At one point I seriously considered dropping out of high school. Moved away from Melba and finished in Houston, Texas where we had family living there. My cousin Michael talked me out of it. We were at a high school basketball game.

Melba had this man living in our house. This guy showed up and started ordering me around. Not only don't I know who my father is, I must deal with this guy. Finally, I told Melba, that either he would leave, or I would leave. She reluctantly Kicked him out the next day. Shortly after, I pretty much couldn't stand being home. I would barely even go home. I stayed with friends mostly. I even slept in my truck some nights. My mom's house, which was once so clean and organized, was that way no more. I joined the US Navy and left Louisiana for good.

PART TWO
METAMORPHOSES
(TO CHANGE STRIKINGLY THE APPEARANCE OR CHARACTER)

CHAPTER 14

MY SCHOOL YEARS

My school years started at a Head Start program in Westlake, Louisiana. I was five years old when I started and graduated when I was 6 years old. The only significant thing to happen at this Head Start program was my breaking the film projector's film. While the movie was playing, I reached up and grabbed the film. I was so fascinated by the way the film went round and round. Of course, it broke immediately, and I was ashamed, briefly. The film was fixed, and the movie continued with further ado.

For the first-grade experiences, I remember nothing but calm.

Although Dexter walks up to my desk one day. He was eyeing my big red apple. When I wasn't paying attention to him, he grabbed it. Then says, "Can I have a bite," as he was taking a bite. All in one determined motion. I yelled out his name, but it was too late.

Dexter set my apple back down on my desk. He laughed as he turned on his heels and walked away. I vowed not to eat that apple, and I didn't. Into the trash it went, the first chance I got. I thought to myself, oh how gross. Learned my lesson and was more careful in the future.

In the second grade, we took a field trip to the dairy company Borden dairy. I was interested in the sense that so many things were moving. I didn't go out much back then because of the racial climate of the time. I remember one day; my mom told me that I wasn't going to school that day. The funeral for Dr. Martin Luther King Jr. was on television. My mom and I watched in silence. She had three pictures on her bedroom wall, (Jesus, President John F. Kennedy, and Dr. Martin Luther King Jr).

While in my third-grade classroom, I would get pulled out to work on my speech. I really liked my third-grade teacher, Mrs. Young. I have already mentioned how I once swallowed a nickel in class. That news traveled so well that Mrs. Young ended up at my home to tell my mom. I learned a lesson that not telling on yourself was the same as lying.

The fourth-grade year in school found me having bullying problems. this kid twice my size decided to bully me every day. I was never one to tattletale about these types of things, no matter what. I dealt with it most of the school year. One day I couldn't take it anymore. I started yelling at him when he would start bullying me around. That brought attention he didn't want. Eventually, he stopped bullying me altogether.

My fifth-grade year was okay. With all the confusion in my young life. I did poorly in my studies, and it came back to hurt me in the end. I did not know how sick my mom was during this period. I ended up failing the fifth grade and had to repeat the grade. Then my mom died later that summer after I failed the grade. In hindsight, as I look back at it all, it was probably for the best. I was better off being held back. Being in the same grade as my sister Paula was not good (she is a year younger than I am). My second go around in the fifth grade went much better. What a difference a year made. I passed on to the next grade a better student (6th grade).

My introduction to sports begins in the sixth grade. By being hand-picked by coach Frusha along with five others. The five others were Troy, Steve, Chris, Mark, and another, I can't remember. I would play baseball and football during that same school year. Jimmy was another simi-bully of mine. It's not a physical threat, but mostly just a nuisance. One phenomenon I noticed was how the girls were outgrowing us boys, or so it seemed.

Teachers warned us in the seventh grade that the eighth grade would be harder than the seventh grade. I thought the 7th grade was the hardest yet. Including the notorious 5th-grade year that I had to repeat. It was the first year that we got equivalence testing on a statewide and perhaps even on the federal level. Turned out to be one of my favorite school years. Oh, and we boys started catching up with the girls in growth. My 7th grade science teacher Mr. Stevens was so much fun. He would come to our physical education classes and play softball with us. Hitting home runs like it was so easy. He would allow us to watch the World Series games on his TV in class. This was when these Major League World Series games would be played in the middle of the day. Mr. Stevens always seemed like he had no stress or worries of any kind.

In my eighth-grade year, we overtook the girls in height and overall size. We were introduced to line dancing and square dancing. I was allowed to attend school dances, which were very chaperoned. At first, the 8th-grade boys were apprehensive to engage with the girls on the dance floor. Little by little, we finally worked up the nerves to join the girls. Playing football for coach Clyde wasn't easy for me. He was very demanding. I didn't make the basketball team in the 7th grade. I did make it in the 8th grade.

My ninth-grade year was enjoyable. My teacher Mrs. Reynolds was my favorite teacher of all my school years. Not because she was easy, it was that she made us all better. Not many teachers have that gift of bringing out the best in students with varying abilities. Those pop quizzes were an effective way to keep us focused. She cared about us all, equally. It was the year before we were to transfer to Westlake High School. I had been at Mossville Jr. High School since the first grade. So many memories to remember and cherish. I would have my first girlfriend during my 9th grade school year. Katrina was so nice and friendly. We were going along beautifully until I messed it up. I admit it was wrong, but I messed around with Lavinia. Destroying the relationship I had with Katrina. I learned a lot from this experience (life lessons). I never again did that again to any female. I made the honor roll a couple of times this year, a first. Wish we could have remained at Mossville Jr. High School, up to our senior year.

Went out for football at Westlake High School for a reason. With all the drama with my birth mother, I needed some way to release aggression. Using the rough physical contact and roughness of football. Although Westlake High School had been integrated five to six years earlier. There were still signs of "Jim Crow Laws" lingering around. A football team is supposed to be a brotherhood. That first year was not anything close to that. I felt unwanted at this school and developed enemy teammates on the football team. All the Caucasian students stayed away from the Afro-American students. We stayed away from them. They took the back of the school, while we had the front of the school. All I know is that I missed Mossville Jr. High School a lot. Yes, Mossville was all Afro-American, and Westlake at one time was all Caucasian. Prior to 1970, Everyone was comfortable with their own kind. But how can a society coexist if you are always segregated? Integration is a good thing in my opinion. Especially if everyone is to be viewed as equal. Just so long as everyone is like-minded on this issue. After all, this is a free country, and to each, their own in my opinion. My 11th and 12th grade years were mediocre academically. My only motivation was joining the military to get out of Louisiana on my own terms.

CHAPTER 15
WHO IS MY FATHER?

Finding out who my father was led to a bizarre twist of events. Can you imagine finding out who your father was at the age of 50 years old? And to find out who you thought were your cousins. Come the find out, they are your siblings. With the father as you. This is exactly how it happened to me. My Aunt Bernadine told my siblings, Larry, Freddy, and Deborah who I really was. My siblings all told me that we were all fathered by Lester "Bob" Ford. If anyone wonders, why I put Ford after my name. This is the reason why I do it. Later, I found out I had two more siblings. A brother and sister who were touching to me the first time I met them in person. Rason and Tesha are my flesh and blood siblings.

Before Melba finally admitted who my father was. I knew it because of my Uncle Herbert and my siblings (via Aunt Bernadine). After which my birth mother

(Melba) finally somewhat told me the truth. It was more like admitting the truth. Only to revert back to denying it vigorously. I told her that my Uncle Herbert was still in high school when I was dropped off at my mom's house. He knew what the truth was back then. Am I to discount what he told me? She just holds her position and asks, "Do they know better than me." I tell her that she has admitted it twice, and she lies and says, "No I did not." I asked Melba, are all these people lying? She says yes, they are all lying. She then goes on and deny that Bob Ford was my dad. With a straight face without blinking an eye. I felt sorry for her and prayed for mercy on her soul. Melba once told both my wife and me the truth again in detail. I was very shocked at how much she had a vivid memory of all that had happened. A couple of years later, Melba goes back to complete denial. Sometimes I feel she might have a mental health issue. I am not qualified to diagnose any medical condition, let alone mental sickness. But one can wonder, and I like most will do that.

I've given up on Melba. She is my birth mother, and I must honor thy mother and thy father. May God have mercy on her soul. I will continue to pray that she repents. I have forgiven her already. I am so thankful that she did not find a way to have an abortion.

My father's widow, Brenda told me how my father knew I was his son.

Apparently, my name came up a lot in their home in New York City. My father specifically said Marvin is my son, many times according to Brenda. He said that I was living down in Louisiana. I can't put all the blame on Melba. I must think that something or somebody kept my father away from me. Back then in the deep south people buried secrets all the time. I really don't know why my father didn't make himself known to me. Guess I will never ever find out about this one major unknown.

All I know is that my father died in 1990 at the age of 60. For whatever reason, I have voided the opportunity to know him as my dad. I know of other family secrets that have been buried also. I will not speak of them in this book. If anyone asks me, I WILL NOT LIE!

I never got to meet all my aunts and uncles on my father's side, except for my Uncle Ernest and many years ago, Uncle Emmitt. Fourteen in all, and I only met two of them. I never got to meet my paternal grandparents on my father's side either. My grandfather lived to be 104 years old and was a remarkable man as I am told. I still have not met many of my cousins on my father's side either. It took 50 years to find out who my father was. I wonder if I will have enough time to meet them all.

I did have the pleasure of being around my father as my uncle in the early to mid- 1960's. I would often sit and watch him barbecue for prolonged periods of time. First, I wonder if there was anything intuitive going on here. Second, he obviously knew that I was his son, why not make it known?

My father and Aunt Bernadine packed up and moved to New York City. It was in the late 1960's when they left Louisiana. I would always be at their house, but that all ended. They lived only two houses down from our house. Hanging out with my protector, Deborah mostly was my biggest loss when they were gone. Freddy and Larry would teach me things as well.

None of us had any idea we were siblings at this time. I was devastated when they moved to Queens, New York. I needed a father without a doubt, but I understand there are and have been plenty of kids who have been through much worse than I have.

CHAPTER 16
THE NEIGHBORHOOD

The neighborhood I lived in was all Afro-American. It was thickly wooded to the point you could not see through the trees. This neighborhood was known as Belaire. It was a rural suburb of Westlake, Louisiana. I lived on 6th street where many things went on. Hunting for things to do was not an arduous task. Playing all sorts of games, like Simon Says. Mostly trying not to get into trouble was everyone's mission. When it became dust-dark, we threw rocks at Bats. I can't think of one successful hit.

Patrick, my best friend, was bullied a lot also. For no particular reason, he was picked on in a hateful way. He was shot with BB guns while minding his own business. Once he got injured when he was roped off the back of a horse, like the real rider. I never understood why they did those things to him. Patrick was a nice kid to everyone. Years later, he went out and got trained in Martial arts. He also became a bodybuilder and got built up muscle-wise. No one ever messed with him again.

Every now and then, everyone was fair game to get bullied. We would have to deal with thugs. The likes of David, Robert, Michael (not my cousin), and others want to be thugs. They would just appear and start harassing whoever was too slow to run to safety (home). In our hood, you either learned the ways of the outlaw thugs or succumbed to their raft. I got beat up many times, and beat up others over the years in our hood. That was just the way it was. Whatever happened stayed untold to your parents. That was the unwritten rule in our hood.

Once there was a young Caucasian lady murdered by one of the thugs from our neighborhood. This was not one of those times when you used the word allegedly. It was real and he did it, so forget the possibility of reasonable doubt. No, this idiot killed this innocent young lady. Word got out that the KKK from Westlake, where the Murder occurred. They were coming to cause trouble, in our Hood (Belaire). Let me just enlighten you on this fact. They knew that we (meaning the hood as a whole) were just as good as they were with guns. Every house had guns and knew how to use them. They drove by a few houses and decided that it was a bad idea.

Good decision on both sides. They caught the guilty party after putting a bullet in his back. I think he is still in Angola Louisiana State Prison, for life. This guy was one of the thugs from our hood that used to rough us up. I cannot say much about the murder since I never had firsthand knowledge.

I got my first gun at age 12 and already had experience with guns prior to that. A single-shot 12-gauge shotgun. Which is probably unheard of in today's thinking on guns and children. At our high school, 50% or more of the pickup trucks had Rifles and Shotguns in the gun racks (in plain sight). My shotgun was in my pickup truck, sitting in a gun rack for all to see. There was not one school shooting...ever. I guess it really isn't the guns. Maybe it is the people and the secular changes since that innocent time when I was growing up.

We would go snake hunting with our shotguns. Our hunting of Rabbits, Squirrels, Raccoons, and anything else that moved. This was a regular thing of ours. Birds were hunted with BB guns and Pellet guns. I once shot a girl with my BB gun. Willy Mae, who was walking down our street toward us. We were just sitting on my aunt Dorothy's porch. I thought I was out of ammunition, (BB's). I was shooting it at my foot and another miscellaneous thing but nothing came out. So, I decided to do something that every gun owner will tell you, the gun is always loaded. So, when Willy Mae got even with us, I shot at her. She made a turn into the driveway of my home, crying. She knocked on our door. Wiping her eyes, I still stupidly didn't get it yet.

Finally, my birth mother called me over and took my BB gun as punishment for shooting Willy Mae. That was a bonehead thing for me to have done. I never, to this day, have aimed a weapon at any person again.

Roaches were in abundance in Louisiana. We had them, especially after my mom died and Melba took over the household. They would get into everything. Not to exclude clothes, kitchen cabinets, and even every inch of walls and floors. I hate roaches, which is probably why I love living out west. We would see roaches outside underneath tree bark and sometimes just flying through the air. I really don't like them at all.

I started driving a manual transmission at the age of 12 years old.

Most of us in the hood could drive, way before the legal age to do so. There always seemed to be an available car or truck around to drive. There were never any police around, so driving was easy to learn. I would drive Patrick's brother's Ford truck. It was a 4-speed manual transmission.

Basketball goals were always up and in heavy use. I played basketball so much; I got really good at it. The rules were always vague, but we managed. Fights were quickly solved to get back to playing. Foul calling was suspect because everyone was their own referee. Calling infractions such as walking, carrying, or packing the basketball was notorious. The bottom line is that we all enjoyed playing the game of basketball and made it work; despite the extra jabbing at each other.

We played tag football whenever the Louisiana heat would allow it. For some reason, football always kept us civil. It was more organized than basketball was. Never any fights and arguments were few and none. The rules were more steadfast and easier to stick with. And understanding that the faster players were your main priority. Like Jasper and Michael (my cousin), you had to try and contain them two for sure. The area we played at on the street was marked off to about 45 yards (goal line to goal line).

Basically, telephone pole to telephone pole with three catches equaling a first down. The only thing that kept the fast guys in check was the width of the street (narrow). Big Stef, is the future high school and college offensive lineman. Was a handful even back then. He was the biggest dude out there and the strongest. I tried to avoid him for the most part, but every so often I would get it handed to me. Playing tag football was a thrill.

CHAPTER 17
MY SPORTS EXPERIENCES

Little league baseball was the thrill of my sporting experience. The only way I was able to play baseball was because it was free. Melba could not afford it, and of course, I had no father. I loved all our players. We got along well together as a group. Playing baseball also helped me get away from my confused home life. That first season did not go well as far as winning goes, but it was fun. We lost every single ballgame that first season. The other team had nice uniforms, while ours were outdated. We looked like a 1920s-era baseball team. The following season, we chose to wear white T-shirts and blue jeans. We were laughed at in the beginning. That ended quickly when started beating the exact team from the year before. We won every single ballgame convincingly. I caught the last out in right field. I'll never ever forget that hot and humid summer night in 1972.

Recreation football was Bellaire versus Mossville, with Bellaire being the underdog. Mossville beat us every time we played. We did ok the following year, but it was nothing to call home about. They were just dominating in every phase. So, 1972's team was a disaster and so was the 1973 Bellaire team. The good thing was that both teams combined forces as we all played for the school team. The Mossville Jr. High School Pirates: if you can't beat them, you join them. Coach Clyde was a good coach, but there were issues. One issue was that he did not like me. Deep down, I thought it was because I was fatherless. Once, I missed a block in a game.

Kerry got blown up on the play for a huge yardage loss. At half-time, Coach Clyde punched me in my stomach, for missing that block. It instantly cut my breathing, meaning I lost my breath. He told me I better never let that happen again. Then a few games later he did the same thing to a good friend of mine, Norman (Big C's). Norman quit immediately after having his wind cut, just as it happened to me. I didn't quit for two reasons. One reason was that Coach Clyde could not compare to my step-grandfather's treatment of me. In other words, I got a lot worse years earlier from Alide Jack I. The second reason was that I needed football. I was dealing with not having a father and a confusing life. Norman had a mother and father in his life. He had structural and completeness. I was confused all the way from my birth to that moment. I got a lot of ridicule from Coach Clyde but never was broken by him or anyone else.

My basketball experience consisted of only playing at Mossville Jr. High School. I was picked with several other kids by the coach in the 6th grade. It was important for me to play sports whenever possible. It seems to keep me less likely to become depressed. Not much happened in that 6th grade year in basketball. We basically were learning how to play the game. We got a new coach in my 7th grade basketball season, coach Clyde. On the first day of tryouts, I was the first one cut from the team. I was shocked since I had played the season before. It was an unbelievably unpleasant experience at first. Then I set out to prove Coach Clyde wrong. I played every pickup game I could find. My shot got a lot better, along with my ball-handling skills. When the 8th-grade basketball tryouts came up, I was ready. I was determined not to be the worst player on the court. I ended up making the team, as a second-string bench player. With coach Clyde, everyone played at some point. There was one game where he started the second string. He was teaching the other team a lesson about rough play in the previous game with them (W.W. Lewis). It seems like they were trying to hurt our players and we were not getting any calls from the Referees. It made the game closer than it should have been, but we still won the game. Anyway, our second-stringers were on the court to start the game against their starters. Coach Clyde had us do full-court pressure the whole 1st quarter. We second-string players wore them down. Then the coach put our 1st string into the game. The look on the other teams' faces was disbelief! Our best year was in my 9th grade basketball season. One victory away from winning the championship. The highlight from that year was beating Pearl Watson! They were our biggest competition. The worse highlight was losing to Pearl Watson, for the championship. The coach had promised us that he would give us our game warmups if we won the championship game against Pearl Watson. We did not win, and he did not give us the game warmups. In 1977, Half of us transferred from Mossville Jr. High School to Westlake High School. The other half transferred to Sulphur High School. Football in high school for me was basically as a practice player. Every practice was a game for me, in my way of thinking. Which was fine with me, since my goal was to get throw my wrecked life. I played almost all of the three years I was on that Westlake Rams team. One game in my senior year, we were getting beaten up badly. I went up to our head coach and asked him if I could play. He immediately said no before I could explain why I was asking.

I probably got into maybe one varsity game my whole three years there. It wasn't that the coach said no, it was how he said it. As if I had discussed him. Something clicked in me and caused my blood to boil. I quit a couple of games after that game. Which ended up being St. Louis 30 and Westlake 6. Coach called me into his office a few days later and asked me to finish my senior year. I said no, and that I had earned the right to play at that moment. Right before spring practices, prior to my senior season. Coach flagged me down one day and jumped in my case for skipping off-season weightlifting and conditioning. I had told him that my family was poor, so I had to work and help my birth mother. This man looked me straight in my eyes and said that they were going to get me in spring practices. That fired me up more than anyone could ever know! I went into spring practices with a major chip on my shoulders. Every one of my teammates was now my enemy. I felt like I had a bullseye on my back. I had the best practices I had ever had in my whole football experience. I was blowing up starters, bigger and stronger players than I. I think this angered my head coach so much that he would never play me. No matter what! I was not the fastest or strongest, but no other receiver could outblock or catch better than I. That's why I reacted that way when the coach rudely said no to me playing in that blowout game. I feel that I did plenty in practices in my senior season. I don't have hurt feelings about any of it. I got what I really needed from high school football. An outlet from my family issues.

CHAPTER 18

THE HIGH SCHOOL YEARS

The high school years were okay, thanks to sports. It took a shorter time for us athletes to adjust to a new school. I have no idea what it was like for regular students. In my lifetime, there had been only one single race in schools I had attended. It was a much different time than today. Not that Westlake High School was racist; it was still sort of a new concept for everyone. "On May 17, 1954, every single justice decided that racial segregation of children in public schools was unconstitutional, which meant that separating children was wrong." National Geographic Kids (The road to school desegregation). In the South, this did not even come close to being adhered to at the time of its passing in the high court. In the part of Louisiana where I grew up, segregation lasted until the late 60's or early 70's.

That's 16 years after that unanimous decision came

down in 1954. Mossville Jr. High, (An all-Afro American school) opened a year after this decision in 1955.

Before the Civil War (1861 – 1865), enslaved children were not allowed to attend school." Tonya K. Grant (The road to school desegregation). The town of Mossville was founded in the year 1790. Free Afro-American families started this town under a man this town was named Mr. Moss. The School, Mossville, has a lot of rich heritage engrained in its name. I am proud to have attended there. This town survived the Civil War and much more. There is a museum located in the city of Lake Charles, Louisiana. When a chemical plant took over most of the town of Mossville and all of Belaire, it was a major thing. I contacted the news outlet for 60 minutes to do a story on the history of Mossville, Louisiana. Because of a documentary I had seen about the history of Mossville. They never pursued this amazing American history.

"Then in 1868, congress passed the 14th amendment to the constitution, which guaranteed every citizen equal rights and Protection under the law – including equal access to education." Tonya K. Grant (The road to school desegregation). This of course never happened in Louisiana at the passing of this 14th amendment. Even though this Amendment was passed three years after the end of the Civil War. I often wonder just what our government does in Washington DC. Do state rights supersede federal law? From 1868 to 1970 is a long time apart, 98 years apart to be exact. When I got to Westlake High School, I found out that we were all just human beings. We got along with our Caucasian counterparts great. Just kids with different skin colors, in my opinion.

Jim Crow laws somehow superseded everything our federal government passed. In southwestern Louisiana where I grew up, "The Jim Crow Laws," ruled (to a lesser degree). Starting in the 1870s, Jim Crow laws were the law of the land, in the South. As a result of this, Mossville Jr. High School has opened for Afro-American-only students. Before then the only option Afro-American students had was schools in Lake Charles (Prior to 1955). And a one-room school in the town of Mossville. Westlake High School was open to only Caucasian students. So about 100 years after the start of the Jim Crow laws, desegregation for Mossville students began.

At Westlake High School, there was no fighting that I knew of. It was our school now, so we embraced it. Why not, life isn't perfect. We went to their school in their city. I think overall, everyone made the best of it.

PART THREE
QUO VADIS

(WHERE ARE YOU GOING?)

CHAPTER 19
JOINED THE MILITARY

"Stand Navy out to sea, fight our battle cry! We'll never change our course so vicious Foe's steer shy-y-y-y!"

"Roll out the TNT, anchors aweigh! Sail on to victory, and sink their bones to Davy Jones, Hooray!"

In the year 1979, while still in high school. I became a sworn-in United States Navy Sailor. One of my classmates asked me why did I join the military, and I said to get out of Louisiana. He then asked me wasn't I afraid of getting killed. I answered him with an "I'd be honored to give my life for my country." He didn't get it, because he did not know anything about my confused life. The last worry on my mind was losing my life, so be it if or when that happened. To put distance between myself and my birth mother was worth the challenge of the unknown. I had had enough of all the lies and denials of truth. I still did not know who my father was. Why?

I arrived in San Diego, California for boot camp in August of 1980. My recruiter offered me two other locations for boot camp. I simply asked him which one was further away from Louisiana. San Diego, California, beat out Chicago, Illinois, and Orlando, Florida. I love the state of Louisiana, where I grew up. I am 100% Louisiana with roots that extend all the way back to slavery. On my paternal grandmother's side. They started in Georgia (her mother and grandmother). Her (father and grandfather's side) came from Kentucky. Where they were all slaves. The two sides met in Louisiana through my grandmother, born in 1890, and my grandfather native to Louisiana. My father's father was born in 1874 (Died in 1978 at 104 years old). On my grandfather's side, they were enslaved I Marksville, Louisiana (just outside of Alexandria, Louisiana). I am of Creole descent, because of my paternal side. You can take the boy out of Louisiana, but you can never take Louisiana out of the boy. It was important to me to explain this little history, to ensure my love for my home state. I did not leave Louisiana because of Louisiana. I left Louisiana because of circumstances.

I came with an eyelash of joining the United States Marine Corps first. I was almost a Marine but came to my senses at the last minute. Glad I did since my Naval career was rewarding in many ways. I do wonder what if sometimes, could I have been a "Jar Head"? Anyone who would ask me where I was from. I would proudly say Louisiana!

Navy boot camp was nothing like I expected it to be. Lots of marching. We stood at attention and parade rest a lot too. We did pushups and had to memorize the "eleven general orders." We got tested often on these memorized orders. Get it wrong and you would have to pop down and give our Company Commander 50 pushups. I got called into his office once. I knocked, and stepped in when told to, nervously! I gave my name, Airman recruit Alexander reporting Sir! All at attention with my eyes looking straight forward. Then my mistake; company "(190) One Nine O." My CC (Company Commander) said, recruit Alexander O is a letter. Then he said zero is a number. He then ordered me to pop down and give him 50 pushups. Each one counted out as, 1 sir, 2 sir, 3 sir… all the way to 50. To this very day, I never use the letter O as a number. We also did a lot of class time in boot camp. In San Diego, the US Navy Recruit Training the command was a jacent to the US Marine Recruit Training Depot. We would be in class and this Marine company running. Later, we would go out and run our little mile and a half. Back in the classroom, we would see that same Marine company still outrunning. At boot camp gradu-ation, I was so proud of myself. Went home on leave and ran straight to the Citizen's house. I was not in a good place with my birth mother. Especially since

Melba had sold my Pickup Truck and shotgun and got rid of my dog. Just in the brief time that I was away at Boot Camp. I was really upset with her for doing all of this without any courtesy to inform me first. Her excuse was, "I needed the money."

My first job in the Navy was as a Plane Captain. Turned out, I was good at this type of work. I got certified as a Plane Captain quickly. Over Sailors who had been there long before I got to VAW-112. And they had not been certified yet. We had the E-2C Hawkeye early warning aircraft. I was so happy that Nickel 601 had my name on the nose landing gear doors. AN (Airman) Alexander PC (Plane Captain, I was responsible for this airplane. Those other guys got motivated and got certified as Plane captains quickly. They didn't like being told what to do by a new sailor.

Everyone called me "Baby Al," since I looked very young. Hazing was a thing in the Navy when I joined. When I got word that I was now a certified Plane Captain, I was jumped for hazing. I'm sitting in the shop surrounded by a bunch of Line personnel. My supervisor (Smitty) announces me as PC Alexander. Then I got jumped on and my shirt was pulled up over my head. Each one of them took turns holding me down while the others were slapping my bare stomach. It hurt so bad; that I could barely breathe. In the end, it was done to everyone at some point. We all became brothers and bonded after this hazing thing. After shellback day, which occurs whenever a Navy ship crosses the international date line. You are a Polly Wog until you successfully make it through this brutal ritual. Then you are a Shellback for life.

I was sent to do my "(EMI) Extra Military Instruction." I got sent to the gallery as a pot washer. I hated this job so much, but hey somebody had to do it. Then it was off to the Ships Scullery, where the dishwashing duties are performed. Guys made homemade wine once, but I wanted nothing to do with that. I wanted to get back up to the flight deck and my plane. Six weeks later I was done with EMI forever.

My Plane, nickel 601 was waiting for me. All was right in the world again. A PC in our shop called me over to the blue hole one day. We had an argument, and it went there. First, the blue hole was where the blue shirts worked out. But they were never there most of the time. Back in the day, when we had a problem, we settled it in the blue hole (fighting). His name was Permenter, an ex-boot campmate of mine. Once in the blue hole, it was on. I swung at him and missed, and he hit me on my chin, and I went straight down to the deck. I didn't know that my friend Hadley had followed us into the blue hole. As I attempted to get up, Hadley punched Permenter. So hard, he flew backward and got up and left. Permenter was in my boot camp company as I stated above. We had always been good friends until this. After this fight, we made up about a year later. I told him that he had a nice left cross! He said that Hadley must have boxed before. I informed him that Hadley was from Philadelphia and that they were all boxers.

As a PC, I was really good at it, with a passion. My inspections found a plethora of things wrong on mine and other planes I inspected. I was good at going through flight checks when launching planes on the flight deck.

What a thrill! We oversaw washing the aircraft and applying lubrication afterward. But launching the planes was the best of all of it.

Moved to the airframe shop as an Aviation Hydraulic Mechanic. This was my dream to work on airplanes. It was challenging from day one. Our shop Chief Petty Officer was old school and stuck in his ways. Everyone complained about him except me. To me, This Chief had nothing on my step-grandfather. I took everything he gave with a business-as-usual attitude. They did an evaluation of the Chief and next thing you know; he was gone. The Chief who took his place was a complete hater. Be careful what you wish for. I made Petty Officer Third Class (E-4), which made me feel good about myself. It's not easy to obtain higher ranks in the Navy.

Next thing I know, I'm sent on assignment for "Extra Military Instruction" (EMI). I protested this since I had already done it onboard the ship. One thing about the Military, it follows never on a straight line. Is more like a Roller Coaster.

My TMI assignment ended up being a blessing in

disguise. I was sent to report to the Final Inspection Team. A job that only lasted 6 hours a day. We did jobs like checking to make sure that the landing gear came down before landing. We used binoculars to spot anything wrong with these planes. We also checked to make sure that the landing gear was stored with closed landing gear doors. My favorite job by far was troubleshooting aircraft just before takeoff. I inspected many diverse types of aircraft such as The A-5, F-4 Phantom, F-14 Tomcat, A-4, and E-2C Hawkeye. Just to name a few. It was during this time that my birth mother came out for a visit. My brother Billy also came down from San Francisco, California. It was Melba's first time ever in the state of California. She was overly excited about this visit. Luckily, I had an apartment with another sailor buddy of mine, Tony. It was good to spend time with them both. I had an easy EMI assignment so that made it less stressful. After 6 weeks of this nice and easy assignment, it was time to return to my Squadron. Reported to my First-Class Petty Officer, AMS1 Bradstreet. He informed me that I was being transferred to the Corrosion Control shop.

Corrosion Control was a whole unique experience compared to Airframes. I got sent to Corrosion Control school, then back to my squadron. We painted planes, removed corrosion from our planes, and did many other jobs. My supervisor, Petty Officer Second Class Krinop, was a Kool dude and a short-timer. Meaning Krinop was getting out of the Navy soon. It was a stress-free shop and we all got along. I had the Idea in my head that I needed a break. So, I spent one year away from the Navy. I was still on active reserve, so it was like I never left. Just before I left, the movie "Top Gun" began filming on our base (Naval Air Station (NAS) Miramar San Diego). I wasn't interested in it, so I pretty much stayed to myself as I prepared to return to Louisiana.

My sister Paula flew into San Diego to drive back to Louisiana with me. I took her sightseeing and showed her off to some of my Navy friends. I took her to a San Diego Padres (MLB) baseball game. I ended up drinking too much beer. This forced my poor sister into the driver's seat. The driving trip went well, except for one flat tire in Deming, New Mexico. Stopped in Houston Texas to visit with my beloved Aunt Bernadine. My Aunt Dean, as we called her, insisted I take a nap. I was glad I did as she suggested. The last leg to Lake Charles, Louisiana was a breeze.

Stayed at Melba's trailer home before going to Texas to work on the Railroad. Moved back to Louisiana and stayed with Patrick for a while. I just could not settle down in my home state. I knew where I belonged, back in the US Navy. I missed the adventures of seeing the world. In my mind, I believed that this time I'd retire from the military. I packed up and re-enlisted in the US Navy. During the requalification process, I was elite. Ran the mile in a half in under 9 minutes. Way below the qualifying time. Back in high school on the football team. Backs and receivers had to run the mile in six minutes and fifteen seconds or less.

Back to the grind, without to-sea training exercises Onboard the USS Kitty Hawk. I get reacquainted with "General Quarters," which is sounded off in case of an attack or emergency. "General Quarters verbalized three times preceded by loud bell rings. Then, all hands man your battle stations." This took some getting used to again. Then the stressful "Broken Arrow," warning that was not a drill. When they called Broken Arrow, this meant everyone had to hit the deck spread eagle (arms and legs spread apart, palms up). Broken Arrow was the movement of Nuclear or Secret weapons, all of which were top secret. If you did not get on the deck and spread eagle, the Marines would knock you down with the butt of an M-16!

I got sent to the F-14 Tomcat fighter aircraft school. To prepare for my rate of AMH (Aviation Mechanic Hydraulics). I reported to my new squadron VF-211 (The Fighting Checkmates). The first dude I encountered in my new Airframes shop was Lex, Danny Ferry. He is better known as "Fighter Lex." He started working on me from the start. All I would tell him was that I was from 6th Street. He was from Philadelphia, with the accent to go along with it. He and I would go on to become incredibly good friends. I loved working on the airplane because it was exciting. The f-14 (The same aircraft in the movie Top Gun) was a badass fighter jet. Our Pilots were very Kool, and top-notch at what they did.

Just before the world cruise took off, I almost missed ship movement.

I Overslept that morning and barely made it aboard the ship on time. Once aboard a ship and knowingly in trouble, I was ordered to put my uniform on (dress blue Crackerjacks). I had to go to the Head (restroom) and ran right into Master Chief Gaylor, a very mean man. He yells at me to go and put my God damn uniform on NOW! Without missing a step, I asked him if I could take a leak first. His answer had us laughing for years, which was HELL NO! Lex and I made a song about this whole scene:

The United States Navy is the most powerful force in the world!

The Oreo boys (somewhere in the Indian Ocean)
-Master Chief-
"Petty Officer Alexander Get your uniform on Now!"
-Marvin-
"Yeah, uh yes Sir Master Chief, can I take a piss first?"
-Master Chief-
"WHAAAAA! YOUR GOD DAMN UNIFORM $#hz

"Oh Shit"

**You thought you'd sleep late, but you ran outta luck!
You got caught on the bridge, now you're trick
fucked! They took you to Mass to see the CO. You
walked outta there without your Crow. And let's not
forget that you disobeyed an order, 45 45 bread, and
water!
HAY! Get your damn uniform on NOW! Master
Chief, can I take a piss first?
Hell no, Get back in there now!
(I did go to captain's mass but only got a 6-month
suspended sentence...and not 45 days in the brig on
bread and water)**

During my first WestPac (Western Pacific) cruise after my year off, I was ready. I worked my butt off in Air Frames. For a reason that I'm not sure of or know of. I was put into Corrosion Control again. I just laughed it off and did my thing, as if I had a choice. Later, on this cruise, I became an AMH 2 (A Second-Class Petty Officer (E-5). After doing very well on the advancement examination. Our First-Class Petty Officer left the squadron shortly after the end of the WestPac cruise. I became the supervisor, and I accomplished a personal goal of becoming a leader of men. Our shop became #1 in our squadron. We got things done that weren't even possible. How you might ask, by doing whatever was necessary. Never any excuses were accepted. Even complaints are not accepted. I embraced the moment in every way, as our shop produced. I had a studio apartment located in downtown San Diego. Life was great, with some of the most beautiful women on planet Earth. Lex and I were joined by Patrick and Rubio. As we lived the life of a single and free life. Patrick actually moved out of Louisiana just after I returned from the world cruise. Later his little brother Chris joined him in San Diego. We all had motorcycles, I had two of them. It was a fun time to be young and single. Then one day, it all came to a sudden end.

I met my future wife, Kelli. Introduced to me by my sister from another mother, Shawna (a super individual). I thought nothing of it at first, but things, should I say, materialized. To this day, I consider Shawna my true sister. She is such a good person. Her daughter, Jessica, calls me Uncle Marvin still to this day. I always said that I would never get married while still in the military. So, I got married and left the US Navy for good after 10 years of service (8 actual active duty and counting the swearing-in while still in high school and the year of inactive and the year of active reserve). On my exit interview with my Commanding Officer, I was told how much they wanted me to stay in. He offered to frock me to First Class Petty Officer (E- 6). If I extend for one year. I often wonder what my life would have been like if I had stayed until retirement. I only had 10 years to complete it.

**The Navy Song "Anchors Aweigh": Anchors Aweigh,
My Boys, Anchors Aweigh!**

FAREWELL TO FOREIGN SHORES WE SAIL AT
BREAK OF DAY-AY-AY-AY.
THROUGH OUR LAST NIGHT ASHORE, DRINK
TO THE FOAM, UNTIL WE MEET ONCE MORE,
HERE I WISH YOU A HAPPY VOYAGE HOME!
Blue of the mighty deep, gold of god's great sun.
Let these our colors be, till all of time be done-n-n-
ne.
On Seven Seas we learn Navy's stern call.
Faith, courage, service true, With honor over, honor
over all

CHAPTER 20
1ST MARRIAGE

I got married to Kelli Edington on August 26, 1989. Only several months before leaving the US Navy. We purchased a condominium in Escondido, California as a newlywed couple. While in Escondido, we fostered twin boys (Tim and Terry). Melba would come for a visit, and all went well. They brought a whole different type of experience. We would eventually adopt the twin boys and make them our very own. Due to safety concerns, we had to move. We moved to a home in Mira Mesa, a suburb of San Diego, California. Then came our daughter (Whitney), who we would also adopt.

The move to another home in Mira Mesa was made for our new business venture. "A Unique Boutique," where we sold pottered and canvas art. Julie, Kassi, Gerry, Kelli, and I all moved into this very large home. It had a pool (with a diving board) and a jacuzzi. This arrangement wore out eventually. Everyone went their separate ways. We enjoyed it while it lasted. The excuse was that the house was haunted. I had never seen anything at all.

Our next move was to Valley Center, California. On a four-plus acre property, which the kids absolutely loved. They played for hours on the big wheel three-wheelers. Used the jacuzzi as a pool somehow. I bought a basketball goal for the kids that would end up lasting their whole childhood. We went on many camping trips, where the boys got hooked on fishing. But all good things must come to an end. Kelli got a job offer in Chicago, Illinois. Being a truck driver, I could work anywhere.

It was off to the suburb city of Arlington Heights, Illinois. While moving into our new home, I broke my wrist. Great, but being a role model for my boys, I continued to unload the Moving truck. My wrist, as I found out later, was badly broken. It was worth it for many reasons, to show strength to my boys. It was a shock to us to find out just how many snowstorms occurred that first winter. Not to mention the extreme cold. The twins have a successful Little League baseball season. We adopted a new dog and named him Lucky! Turned out to be a very good dog. Then came the purchase of our second home. In South Elgin, Illinois, where we would raise our kids.

Moving in day was so rewarding for all of us. The kids were so happy, and this little Village was perfect.

Yes, in the Chicagoland area, these small towns are known as villages. Tim and Terry would go on to become very good at baseball. My daughter Whitney would go on to be exceptionally good at Art. So good in fact, that she was turned down by an Art instructor. He said that Whitney was more advanced than him. He said that he would not be able to help someone that advanced. Whitney, Terry, and Tim had a happy upbringing and gave me completeness.

My kids had busy childhoods. They played sports of their choice.

They put up with their father, LOL! Took up Karate and made it all the way to being awarded a yellow belt. We did a lot of camping and fishing. We lived in a neighborhood where it was safe for them to ride their bikes all over the place. Tim took up singing in the school choir, I was very proud of him. We enjoyed the Ballet, and the Nutcracker almost every single year. All my kids were avid readers and checked out library books every Sunday. They kept up with their grades in school, for the most part. Although there were some setbacks along the way. From where they came from, developmentally, they did a wonderful job catching up with their age group. It was an immensely proud moment when Tim and Terry graduated from High School. They were the first class at their brand-new high school to march down the Aisle. I never got that opportunity to march down the Aisle, so this was special for me. I finished high school at summer school.

Got my diploma after completing summer school. I have no excuses for this, except having a lack of effort. At some point in my senior year, I had completely given up on finding out who my father was. I would drop the subject for over thirty years.

Tim and Terry were independent and working two jobs. They entered classes at a junior college. My wife Kelli was getting over a cancer scare, and I was working as a Linehaul truck driver. All was not as well as it seemed. One day Kelli came into our bedroom to let me know that she and my daughter Whitney were moving out. For several years prior to this, Kelli had been threatening me with divorce. I thought Tim Terry and I would be kicked out. We kept a suitcase packed just in case. This was a surprise, despite all the threats. We ended up getting a divorce and to this day, I don't understand why. What in the heck does irreconcilable differences mean? This broke up our family for no good reason. I have to take the blame because I was the head of the household.

My meeting another woman might have pushed the divorce into hyperdrive. Her name was Laura, a blonde-headed green-eyed Russian Jewish lady. It was a wild romance that was like a roller coaster. My daughter Whitney didn't like Laura, and the twins weren't too keen on the idea either. Laura moved into our home, and it did not go well.

Unbeknownst to my kids, I allowed Laura to move in because she told me that she was pregnant with our baby. Laura brought her two daughters to live and move in. Grettalisa and Fionagrace and I fell in love with these beautiful little girls. My birth mother was also living with me temporarily as she waited for her new place to be ready. While having this mostly sexual experience with Laura, I cared for a complicated household. I was also dealing with my daughter, who was suffering from anxiety and depression. I was running around with my head in a cloud. Got a little break when I was invited to travel to Kansas City, Missouri. It was a chance to win a brand- new Semi truck. I was a finalist in this random contest I had entered. I took Laura along on this trip. We stayed in a 5-star hotel and were wined and dined extremely well. This trip really took a lot of stress off me. I thought this would be a turning point in my life.

The forecast for this Tuesday, February 9, 2010, was blizzard-like conditions. On Monday, the day before, I had been shut down in Indianapolis, Indiana because of heavy snow and whiteout conditions. It was already snowing when I left Chicago, Illinois for Indianapolis. A week earlier, Whitney and I had an argument (disagreement mostly). It was over her doing Roller Derby, of all things. I had told her that I could not sit in the stands and watch someone hurt her. The point here is that without knowing that this would be the last time I would see Whitney alive. I did not hug her when I left for work. I just left her on the steps of her mom's apartment. Hug your loved ones every chance you get.

Take my word on this. A few days later, we made up on the phone. The last time I would ever hear her voice again. We always made up; we were close. That put me in a good place.

This last phone call was about how I would be moving back to San Diego, California. We were planning how she would be joining me there after her graduation from high school. On the night of February 9th, 2010, I get a call from my son Tim. He told me that Whitney tried to kill herself. I hung up with him and got over to our Indianapolis terminal. I told them what had happened and got a load right away. While waiting, I found out that it wasn't an attempted suicide. My baby girl was dead, by taking her own life. I will never tell you how it happened. So please never ask. I asked my son what happened, and he did not know. So, he put Kelli on the phone. She told me that my daughter had come home terribly upset. Locked herself in her bedroom for a long time before Kelli checked on her. The fire department was called, and they busted the door open, and my daughter was unresponsive. They tried to revive her but failed. I drove all the way from Indianapolis to Chicago in a snowstorm. Knowing that my precious little girl was no more. There was nothing I could do about it. I did not blame Kelli or her doctor for lowering Whitney's depression medication.

WHY? Because what good would it do? My baby girl was gone, I was numb. I am still numb and am still trying to come to grips with it all. I could not eat for days. Sleep was not happening either. Laura tried to comfort me, but that didn't help at all. My daughter's funeral was a blur. Part of my long phone conversation with my daughter, a week earlier was how I was going back to San Diego. She was to come and join me later.

I don't remember how long I was out of work, on bereavement leave. All I know is that I only lasted a couple of days. Then I put my two weeks' notice in. I packed up my things on a moving truck and hit the road with my dog Rex. Oh, and Laura and I broke up while I was en route to San Diego, California. I grew up in Louisiana and lived in Chicago for a good many years. But San Diego is where I have spent most of my life, and I consider it home.

CHAPTER 21

2ND MARRIAGE

Back in beautiful San Diego again. I stayed at my childhood friend's house temporarily. It was good to be back home in my familiar surroundings. One day while at a place called Café' Tazza, coffeehouse & Bistro. I met my future wife and soulmate, Claudia. I offered to buy her whatever she wanted. She and I sat and talked for hours. I could not believe how much Claudia and I had in common. This chance meeting turned into a full-blown relationship. She epitomized the meaning of a lady. The way she carried herself in a graceful manner. Her smile was intoxicating. Her hands were extremely feminine in a small size. They had no blemishes of any kind. She dressed modestly in an almost full-length dress. Her breast was covered perfectly without totally covering them up.

Claudia's hair was naturally streaky blonde brown and very long. Her eyes were vivid green with a dark ring around each eye. Making her eyes easy to look into them. My Claudia was a beautiful Latina woman, with strong Spanish roots. She looks like a person who could be from many different countries. I fell for her not long after meeting her over a brief period. We did the old-fashioned courting of no relations until a certain time or when we were both ready. Which lasted many months, as we got to really know each other.

Claudia and I got married in Las Vegas, Nevada. My birth mother and Claudia's kids, Cristian, and Paulina, were in attendance. The Chapel of the Flowers is where the wedding took place. I highly recommend this Chapel! We partied in Vagas and had a blast. Claudia was my beautiful wife and I, her husband. Everything from that point on was right in every way.

Marriage number two was at Corpus Christi Catholic Church in Bonita Vista, California. My wife planned this wedding in less than two months. I was amazed at how it all turned out. Most of the backyard was covered with a large canvas tent. We had a D.J. playing our favorite tunes. The Taco Man was a big hit as well. Both Terry and Tim were there, along with their friends from Chicago. Vince, Charlie, and Anthony who all three were my son's childhood friends. My wife's family welcomed me with open arms. My view of them is good-hearted people who make me feel loved. Mr. and Mrs. Esquer have been nothing less than a mother and a father to me.

Then the trips started happening. Claudia and I

went up to Seattle, Washington. We spent some great bonding time with our son Tim. The highlight of our visit with Tim was "Pikes Market." That was a wonderful experience with our son. Oh, and in our family, all our kids were our kids. This means Paulina and Cristian were not my stepkids, they were my daughter and son. Same with Tim and Terry to Claudia. They were her two sons…period.

Our next trip was to Hawaii, with the younger kids. Terry and Tim were unable to go with us. They, being in the US Navy, prevented that from happening. This trip was so much fun for all of us. I will remember this trip for many years. Driving all over the Island to experience the locals.

Snorkeling amongst all the tropical fish and coral reefs. Pearl Harbor was a very somber experience for us all. It is a must in my opinion.

Louisiana was a trip that was dear to my heart. In preparation for this trip, I had to teach the kids how to say yes sir, no sir, yes ma'am, no ma'am, and Mr. and Mrs. They had never been down south before, except for Florida once. Cristian and Paulina did a fantastic job. They got compliments from Kay and Elray, my Citizen people. They got to see live Alligators and other animals. We stopped at a restaurant in Beaux Bridge, Louisiana. On our way to New Orleans. The Kids got to eat frog Legs, boiled Crawfish, Alligator, shrimp, and Crawfish Etouffee. New Orleans was a fun time for us all. We dined at the famous "Café Du

Monde" in the French Quarter. This Café has been around since 1862. When you enter, you go back in time.

Everyone seeks the famous "Beignet" except me. I was into the coffee, and it did not disappoint. We headed to Baton Rouge, next to go see the LSU fighting Tigers play a college football game. It turned out to be a historic event. It was the first LSU football game to ever be forfeited due to weather. They have been playing college football at LSU since 1893. That was a drag, but we did see the first quarter of action before the severe weather hit. My family, Elray and Kay Margret allowed us to stay at their home. While in Lake Charles, Louisiana they were great hosts.

The Chicago trip was unique in many ways. The kids and I went to a Chicago White Sox baseball game. Cubs versus the White Sox, a matchup with no love lost. We visited with a close friend of mine. Sam and I once worked together in Chicago when I lived there. We went to the famous "Navy Pier." Millennium Park was awesome to see and experience. On one of our vacation days, we drove in three states. They were Wisconsin, Illinois, and Indiana, as we visited the University of Notre Dame. Also, a cheese factory in Kenosha, Wisconsin. We visited Wrigley Field and the surrounding area. We visited my birth mother and helped her get into a better senior residential community in South Elgin, Illinois. She is so happy in this new place, where the care is excellent. It gave me peace of mind to know that Melba was taken care of.

My near-death experience after a reaction to medication. It landed me in the ICU in critical condition. My Claudia and her mother's fast action probably saved my life. While Claudia and I were visiting her mom and dad, my throat started closing. Josefina (Claudia's mother) noticed something was wrong with my breathing. She immediately gave me Benadryl, which later the doctor said may have saved my life. Instead of calling an ambulance, my wife got me into the Navigator and drove amazingly fast to the emergency room. By the time I got there, my throat was almost completely closed. They worked on it right away and ended up spending almost a week in the intensive care unit. I am one lucky man to have such a determined wife.

Terry's surgery trip to "Walter Reed Hospital" a national military medical hospital, in Bethesda Maryland. The same hospital was used by US Presidents. As well as all the military services. The first thing we noticed was all the deer walking around. They would come right up to you. On this trip, it was only Claudia and me. We were there to support our son for a serious surgery. Before his operation, we went to our nation's capital and visited all the sights. My favorite was the Lincoln Monument. I always visit all our war memorials. Terry and I went to a Washington Nationals Major League Baseball game. That was a real treat, since my son and I are big baseball fans. Terry's surgery was a complete success and he recuperated fast.

Even the doctors were amazed. Another successful trip was over, so we returned to beautiful San Diego, CA.

We then flew to Houston, Texas to support our son Terry for his participation in playing on the military baseball team. That was a great feeling to be around all these young military men as they train and play baseball. The games were very entertaining and fun to watch.

We moved to the state of Utah and fell in love with it quickly. After renting for a year. We decided to purchase a home. We found the perfect home with a pool and jacuzzi. Shortly after buying this home, Terry goes into silent mode. Shortly after buying this home, Terry goes into silent mode. He simply stops communicating with my wife and me. To this day, we don't understand why. I call him sometimes to see if he is ok. But I will not force myself on him in any way. He is a grown man, and it is his business. I love him with all my heart, and he knows this. Now we concentrate on our other three adult children.

COVID-19 hits hard and I get it first. I moved to the other side of our home. Claudia does an excellent job of caring for me. At one point I thought

I would not survive this illness. I went four days without eating. I had a headache 24 hours a day. I could not breathe very well at all. She made me get up several times a day. This helped to alleviate fluid buildup in my lungs. I was able to overcome this illness, fortunately. I would go on having symptoms for over a year after catching COVID-19.

My wife caught COVID-19 next and she had it worse than I had it. They wanted to hospitalize her, but we declined. They set her up with Oxygen and our home. She took some powerful COVID medications. Finally, she eventually got better and out of danger. We both dodged a bullet on these two close calls.

Our two dogs must be put down due to old age and cancer. The two dogs were so loved. Rex, our American Bulldog, was such an obedient dog. We did all we could do to stop his pain because it eventually got too bad. Davito, our French Bulldog, was a lovable little dude. All he ever tried to do was please us. He too had cancer that overcame him. We miss these two very much.

I lost my sister and two brothers in less than two years. Larry and Freddy in Houston, Texas, and Deborah in Poughkeepsie, New York. This was devastating to go through for me. I traveled to my brother Freddy's funeral in Houston, with my son Cristian. Not one year later, I'm back in Houston for my Brother Larry's funeral. My wife travels with me, to support me in my loss. Six months later, my wife, Cristian, and I are in Poughkeepsie, New York for my sister Deborah's funeral. I mourned all their deaths in disbelief. It is still a shock to me how this could have happened. I grew up around them all. Not even knowing that we had the same father.

Our next trip takes us on a major road trip. We flew into Dulles Airport in the Washington DC area. Stayed at our incredibly good friends, Debbie, and Bill's home in Virginia. Drive to Allentown Pennsylvania, for my little brother's wedding. Afterwards, my wife the two kids and I all decided to finish my last state to make 50. By driving to the state of Maine. So, we then drove to Portland, Maine. It was a great family moment as we celebrated in the car as we crossed the Massachusetts border into Maine.

We now have a new puppy. She is a Golden Doodle that is adorable. The training stage is underway. She is so cute and draws a lot of attention wherever we bring her. Her name is Lucy, a sweet girly.

CHAPTER 22
A TRUCKER TO THE BONE

I am a trucker to the bone. My heart and soul are put into this occupation. That I would do for free if I could. I embrace everything trucking and respect the road. All my children were in the big truck with me. So, they have a really good understanding of what I do. My wife loves coming out with me as well, especially over the road.

I've been a professional truck driver since 1995. It all started when my good friend Ron Asked me to help him out with his air freight business. He was an owner-operator in the Air Freight trucking business. I really enjoyed this trucking experience. First delivering Air Freight to Customers, then once empty, it was time to pick up Freight. This Freight would be brought back to the warehouse sorting for distribution to air cargo companies. Once the Freight was separated, it was loaded on trucks to be taken to the Los Angeles Airport

(LAX) cargo locations. I was hooked, line and sinker, by this new trucking experience, soon to be a trucker for life. I would go on to attend a truck driving school In the San Diego area.

Where I obtained my commercial driving license (CDL). Then it was time to start looking for a trucking job. I would go on to work in a variety of trucking jobs over the years. Including going into business as an owner-operator.

I've owned four big trucks and have earned a very good income over the years. I gave up being a Real Estate agent, a Stockbroker in training, and a Naval Career. To me, being a professional truck driver was the perfect choice. (My trucking credentials and experience are as extensive as any.

Things like operating a straight truck, dry van, flatbed, refrigerator trailers, a hazmat endorsement, TWIC card (Transportation Worker Identification Credential…for offshore shipping yards/docks) tanker, doubles and triples, and air brakes). Driving a straight truck is kind of like driving a U-Haul truck. But may have air brakes which would require a special license. Dry van trailers simply haul dry freight. Flatbed trailers are specialized freight that's strapped or chained to a flat uncovered surface. The refrigerated trailers carry frozen meats, dairy, produce, and non-hazardous dry freight. Tanker trailers haul fuel chemicals and food stuff. Doubles and triples or plainly two trailers connected or three trailers connected. They can be dry vans, refers, or flatbed trailers. I've driven in all weather, road, and traffic conditions over the years. The two worst weather conditions for truckers in fog and wind. If you cannot see, you are in a dangerous situation. Fog will cause an extremely stressful driving experience. My all-time worst is the wind. The only reasonable thing to do in high winds is to pull over in a safe location. High-profile vehicles are no match for strong gusty winds. Tire chains in snow and icy conditions are just mandatory on mountain grades. Especially when in any downhill or uphill situations.

I would take my twin boys to the biggest trucking show in the United States every year. This trucking show is in Louisville, Kentucky. I would rent a car and drive not far from the Kentucky border with Indiana and get a hotel room for us. This was a special time between my twin boys and me, they got to learn so much about what I did as a trucker. Plus, the opportunity to come away from the show with many freebies. I cherish those times with them.

There is really nothing like trucking in my opinion. Especially when the days of the week simply do not matter. Neither does the time of the day matter. Still the same, truckers are expected to be on time in their pickup and deliveries. No matter what the weather or traffic conditions might be. There are good times as well as tough times. In the end, it is a rewarding occupation. Mainly because there is always a completion or ending of every task. A satisfaction as you await your next challenge. It has turned into a passion for me personally. Being responsible and dependable comes from how I was raised. My mom taught me these important values and more. May she rest in peace. I have always taken safety seriously in my profession. Safety is an attitude more than anything. You either commit to it 100% or be in danger of accidents and injury.

I have encountered many "Lot Lizards" all over the country. They are prostitutes who converge around truck stops. I feel sorry for these young women, as they do this illegal activity. Sometimes they work independently and other times they have a pimp. Now we as truck drivers have a huge responsibility to fight Human Trafficking. It happens at truck stops all over and truck drivers can make a difference. By reporting any unusual activities involving multiple young females in one vehicle. Noticeably young girls, like teenagers, walk around working in an area. If in doubt, call the Human Trafficking hotline at 1-800-373-7888.

I've seen the entire country, all fifty states. Mostly all of the states by way of trucking. As the saying goes, "By any means necessary." I have traveled the country by sea, air, automobile, and by Big Truck! In the summer of 2023, I completed this personal quest of mine. The state of Maine was the last state I had not been to. My wife and two younger kids drove there by car. While at my little brother Rason's wedding in Allentown, Pennsylvania. We decided to go for it and complete my dream of accomplishing all fifty states. We rented a car and drove to Portland, Maine. Basically, I really have seen so much while trucking. In the lower 48 states, I have seen:

State capitols, NASCAR racetracks, Civil War Battlefields, Revolutionary War Battlegrounds, Sports stadiums: NFL, MLB, NBA,

College sports, Volcanos, Mountain ranges...like Mt St. Helens, Mt Shasta, Mt Hood, The Appellation Mountains, Smoky Mountains, Rocky Mountains, The Sierra Nevada's mountains, Mt Rainier, The Poconos mountain ranges, The Blue Ridge mountains, 10,000 lakes in Minnesota, The Great Lakes, The Mississippi River, The Ohio River, The Allegheny River, The Arkansas River, The Colorado River, The Columbia River, The Pacific Ocean, The Atlantic Ocean, The Gulf of Mexico, Chesapeake Bay, Lake Pontchartrain, Calcasieu River, Every major highway, Every major Freeway, Every major toll road, Route 66, Nations Capital, Mt Rushmore, Snoqualmie Pass, Donner Pass, Grants Pass, International Falls Minnesota (the coldest place in the lower 48 states), and much more.

As a truck driver, you will have contact with the police a lot. My encounters with police happened around the whole country. I have had courtroom battles because of citations/tickets I had received. I won most of these battles, with the help of a Lawyer most of the time. There were many battles that never made it to a courtroom. But instead, they were settled right there on the side of the road. I've had shouting matches with the police that ended with a handshake. Took a wrong turn, (GPS foul up) once in the capital of North Dakota, (Bismarck). The police officer yelled at me, and I just remained calm. Finally, he asked me why was I off the truck route, and on a restricted street. I told the officer that I was following my GPS coordinates. He and I talked for a while, but at the end of it all, I just followed him to the proper road. Another similar incident occurred in Columbus, Ohio. This officer was extremely helpful and guided me to where I needed to be. There are good police out there. Take my word that they will help you more than not.

One of my favorite times out on the Big Road is when my wife comes out with me. It turns into a great bonding time for us both. She has been to many states on my trucks throughout the years. The good thing about it is how she loves it out over the road with me. So many memorable moments that have enhanced my life for close to 30 years of trucking. I know I must give it to you at some point. When that is, it's anyone's guess.

My trucking mission statement:

To know my job and execute my duties as a service to my customers.

To maintain my equipment according to company,

state, local, and federal rules, and regulations. To always keep myself and my performance in tip-top condition. To have an exceptional driving performance to meet or surpass all expectations. To continuously improve in my personal and professional life. Also continuing to demonstrate effective communication and listening skills. To know that if I am not successful, the company will not be either. And to produce results and not excuses.

CHAPTER 23

MY TWO DAUGHTERS

My two girls, Whitney, and Paulina. They have brought so much joy and satisfaction into my life. Having a daughter can change a man.

Watching her grow up from a baby to a woman is a very enlightening experience for us men. I have always had a remarkably close relationship with both Paulina and Whitney. Whitney told me everything, because of her trust in me. I know things that no one else ever knew. When it came down to the sex talk. She came to me, which was like an honor. Whitney was on my truck as we headed west through the state of Missouri. The subject of sex came up, which led to a full-blown discussion. We covered everything that I knew. I got back with her later with those things I wasn't sure of.

Every time I left to go to work, Whitney would be there to say goodbye. I can still hear her shy voice telling me how much she loved me. I cannot explain just how much I hold on to those moments. I can still hear her voice to this day. As I would pull out of the driveway, and drive away, she would run alongside me (on the sidewalk). I would hear a faint I love you, Dad, what a moment that was.

In sports, Whitney was very athletic and incredibly good at sports. As a little girl. She would play basketball with her brothers and their friends. No other girls would be in those battles. I noticed early on how she would keep up with boys older than her. I put her on a co-ed basketball team. Co-ed means both boys and girls on the same team. I was totally amazed at how good she was with kids her own age. Whitney was clearly the best player on the court. Then there was girls' softball with her best friend Alex. Alex's Dad Chip was the head coach. Whitney was lights out good and so was Alex. It was an absolute joy watching my daughter play softball. I still remember how happy she was. It warms my heart just thinking of it.

As an artist, Whitney excelled beyond expectations. She would be drawing cartoon characters as she watched them on the television. I'd ask her to see it, and it looked amazingly almost identical to the cartoon character. Whitney once drew a human eye that looked so real, it made me want to touch it to see if it was real or not. Her plan was to move to Japan and learn the language. She was infatuated with the Japanese culture.

We lost Whitney to suicide at the age of 16 years old. It still hurts me every time I wonder what she could have been. She was inseparable and our relationship got closer as time passed. She was an extremely talented young lady, where only the sky was the limit. A part of me died with her that blustery night of heavy snow. I was out of town working, and oblivious to what was going on. Whitney knew that I was stuck out of town. I believe that she protected me by not contacting me before the inevitable. She knew I would have lost my mind knowing I couldn't be there to try and save her.

The problem is, in her state of mind, she did not want to be rescued. I still mourn her death; even though I know she is gone. I buried her in a military National Cemetery. Where I too will be laid to rest with her and my wife. On her interment niche, my name is already etched into the stone entrance plate. Eventually, all three of us will be laid to rest together.

Paulina is my little flower, and we are close. I love her to the moon and back. Paulina is an extremely intelligent and determined young lady. I watched her grow up from a little 5-year-old, into a woman. When she was a little girl, she would love it when I would read to her before bedtime. I loved walking her to school while holding hands. When she had sibling issues with her brother Cristian, it was me she ran to. I would hear her call out, Poppa! Paulina has two fathers, her blood dad, Enrique, and me.

Paulina is all that I have left, as my daughter. I really feel truly fortunate to have her in my life. I can care less about her and me not being blood-related. I love her as my own. Period! When she was little, she and I had a special bond. A bond that has withstood the test of time. She is in college doing exceptionally well academically. I am proud of her hard work and determination. She has a drive that is second to none. I know in my heart that she will be a successful person. Anything she decides to accomplish in life. I am not one to crowd my children, especially when they become adults.

Paulina was a part of the support staff for her high school football team. She was impressed with her job, taking it very seriously. I really like that about her. I'm convinced that she will be a leader someday in the future. She was always on the field first and alert to the players' needs.

There was a rule that none of the supporting staff could date the football players. Paulina never broke that rule. She makes it so easy to be proud of her.

One time, I decided to build Paulina a lemonade stand. I wanted both her and Cristian to help build it. The kids and I went to the hardware store together to get the materials needed. They were involved throughout the whole project. We drew out our building plans and went to work. The kids did most of the painting, for the kid effect. It turned out well. Her first time selling lemonade wasn't good. I had a remedy for that logistical issue. I transported Paulina's

Lemonade stand to the softball fields. There was a tournament going on, and she sold a lot of lemonade. Her little cute smile was contagious as we were all smiling.

CHAPTER 24

MY THREE SONS

My Three sons are all their own men. Each has their own identity, and well as talents. Cristian is extraordinarily talented at photography and sports. I've seen him hit a grand slam home run with ease. He once received a bad snap as the punter. 76 yards later, Cristian was crossing the goal line for a touchdown. In high school, he was a kicker and a punter.

Although being right-handed, he actually kicked and punted with his left leg/foot. It was enjoyable to see Cristian play sports. Especially being a major part of his development in sports.

Cristian also has a really good caring heart. He took the time to accompany me to my brother's funeral in Houston, Texas. That was genuinely nice of him, while in the middle of his college studies. Being exceptionally good at photography, I asked him to take some pictures. His pictures were great and led to a video being made.

Cristian kept us company by joining his mother and me at my sister's funeral in Poughkeepsie, New York. Claudia was unable to attend the reception following the funeral. He stayed by my side the entire time. My sister and I were close, and it shook me up badly. He was a huge help in supporting me through this sad time.

My son Cristian thanks me all the time for all that I did for him in his sports training. It was my pleasure to do it. When he was little, I saw in him a lot of athletic ability. I signed him up for basketball, baseball, and football. He did very well in all of them. I look forward to him becoming successful in whatever he chooses to do.

Terry is very into his own thing type of person. Right now, he has cut off communication with the family. If and when I call him (if he is not out to sea) he might answer. It is what it is really. He will let me rest assured that he is alright. He does not call me or anyone else in our family. No one knows why this is. Since Terry never explained why. I give him his space and just say that it is his business. I love my son just as much as I love his brothers and sister. Hopefully, Terry will someday explain why. He lives in Virginia, where he is stationed on a Naval Aircraft Carrier. I wish Terry good health and success as he nears the end of his Naval career.

Tim is more like me in so many ways. He is a down-to-earth type with extremely low stress. His patience is off the charts. A virtue of his strong character. He has the capacity to tolerate far more than the norm. His daily activities are like sequences in time. Tim is not one to sit around. He is always on the go. He doesn't care to watch sports at all. I jokingly call him unsportsmanlike conduct. He just laughs it off, "like water off a duck's back."

I am impressed with how Tim takes care of his business. He has a Yacht in the Seattle area. He has never told me how he obtained it. I never asked since it is his business. I respect the privacy of all my children. When they do ask for advice, I am careful not to step out of bounds. Tim is a lot like me when it comes to his business and keeping it. Claudia and I visited Tim once in Seattle, Washington. He was there on leave, from his duty station in the country of Bahrain. Tim rented an Airbnb in preparation for our arrival. I was not surprised by this at all. He has not a selfish bone in his body. This makes me enormously proud of him.

Tim told me once how he would not get married while in the Navy. It brought back memories of why I got out of the Navy early. It was to get married to his mother. I also refused to get married while in the military. Tim explained the reason why he made this decision. It was because many friends of his, in the Navy, had had bad marriages. He explained how there have been divorces. There have been children involved also.

Broken homes and families split apart. Tim said that he does not want a divorce.

He went through that with his own parents. Kelli and I got a divorce just as Tim and Terry were finishing their first year in college. The reason both of them enlisted in the US Navy was due to my divorce from their mother. The divorce coupled with Whitney's death made for a lot of stress for Tim and Terry. I hurt them and basically had no answers. Sometimes you just have gone through tough times. So, Tim is battle-tested in some unfortunate situations.

I love my conversations with Tim. He is so calm and levelheaded. We have had our disagreements here and there. Mostly when he was in his teenage years. The older he got, the less we argued. Regarding religion, Tim and I have had some tense moments. Never elevating to anger but spirited still the same. I respect my son's opinion and his opinion. I love all my kids and they love me. You cannot ask for anything more than that. I want to see all of them be successful in life.

PART FOUR
TRANQUILITY
(FREEDOM FROM DISQUIETING OR OPPRESSIVE THOUGHTS OR EMOTIONS)

CHAPTER 25

MY NEAR-DEATH EXPERIENCES

I've had several near-death experiences over the years. Sometimes I feel that many of us don't realize how fragile life can be. There are so many ways to die. It might be an Infinite number. I've heard that if it's your time, you will die that day. Accidental deaths happen a lot to younger kids for many reasons. I understand the meaning of, "Near Death experience."

Going to another unknown reality after dying, then coming back to life. There are plenty of people who have experienced dying and then coming back to life. When I speak of my near-death experiences, mine were different. I never lost a heartbeat or was resuscitated. What I'm going to describe about my incidents are different. I was in danger of dying like drowning before being rescued. Let's just call my experiences close calls.

I was a little kid at around eleven years old. It was

Wednesday on free swim day at the Mossville recreation public pool. At this point, I had only been in the shallow end of the pool. Which was only three feet of water. I was practicing every Wednesday, to learn how to swim. On this particular day, I thought I had it figured out. I was not swimming in the three feet of water section, but I was dog peddling instead. So, I worked up the nerves to walk over to the lifeguard. I told him that I could swim now. His name was Elvis, and he was like a high school student or higher. Elvis told me to swim across the ten-foot-deep section of the pool. I jumped into the pool and used up too much energy just to surface. Once I made it to the surface of the water, I began dog peddling across to the other end of the pool. It was a sunny day, and the pool was packed. As I reached the halfway point, I just sank to the bottom of the pool. As I was underwater, I could see Elvis standing. I guess he was waiting to see if I would swim back up. I know this is not a near-death situation, but if no one has seen me go down. I would have drowned. Elvis dived in and pulled me to safety. After getting thoroughly checked out by the lifeguard, Elvis. I was unceremoniously kicked out of the pool. Note, that before the end of that summer, I was a full-fledged swimmer.

While spending the summer in Houston, Texas with family. My cousin Glen and I were walking through the neighbor's yard. It was a shortcut to home, my cousin Marie's house. As we were walking through this yard, my cousin Glen started running. I yelled at him, asking why he was running.

That's when I heard a dog behind me growling. Not just any dog, it was a German Shepherd. Now it's the middle of a very hot summer day. We are wearing only light clothing. Bare feet with shorts and a T-shirt. When I turned around to face the dog, it closed in fast on my position. I thought I was going to be killed. Once the dog was about to jump onto me. I'm standing there with my fist cocked back. As the dog leaped, I punched it as hard as I could. Striking the dog square in Its forehead. The dog yelped; I screamed a sound I had never heard before. The dog ran back to its doghouse, and I ran for dear life back home (my cousin's house). We would find out later that it was a girl dog who had recently given birth to puppies. The nursing German Shepherd was just protecting her puppies.

My friend Lex and I decided to go surfing during a Hurricane that was occurring down in Mexico. This Hurricane caused <u>exceptionally</u> <u>large</u> waves at all the San Diego, California beaches. I had never surfed in those conditions before. When both of us arrived at the beach, it was at least 12-plus foot-high waves. We went through our normal preparations as we always did. Normally, the waves were 3 to 5 feet, and I was good with that. I went on and decided to go for it. Surfing was so therapeutic to me personally. It was a useful <u>source</u> of exercise as well. Oh, and it was a ton of fun.

We entered the Pacific Ocean determined to conquer the waves.

When heading out far enough to pass the breaks of the waves, just before the waves began. You must avoid being pushed back to the beach by pointing your surfboard down and going underneath each coming wave.

Otherwise, you would never get into position. It was rough, as I made it into position. We called this the ready position, where surfers took turns catching waves. In about 30 feet plus of water, we simply sat on our surfboards and talked. Lex took off first and caught one beautifully. I took the next one and was riding my 12-foot wave as well as I could. Then we headed back out. I was getting brave at this point. That would come back to haunt me later. As I took my next wave, something went wrong, and I got dumped on the back side of the wave I just took. The problem was, I drifted too far toward the beach in about 20 feet of water. Right where the powerful waves started breaking downward. I got caught in this and lost my sense of direction. I started swimming where I thought was toward the surface. It was not the surface; it was the bottom. I hit the sand-covered bottom after swimming about 10 feet the wrong way. I was almost out of air when I went to kick off the bottom to start swimming back up. Just then a huge wave went above me and caused me to miss the bottom. I now had to swim 20 feet to get oxygen, or I was going to drown. I really don't know how I survived. About 5 feet from the surface, I ran out of air in my lungs. I was beginning to start breathing in water in place of air when I broke the surface. I thought I was going to die. I got to the top and coughed up water, after taking in much-needed air. Some surfer dude was nearby and only said "Far out man." Once I was ok to move again, I headed for the beach. I told Lex I was done and that I almost drowned. I got dressed and headed straight to Sick Bay on base. I surfed again after that many times, but no more high surf stuff. This was a close call and I feel very lucky.

Onboard the USS Ranger CV-61 while on a deployment in the Indian Ocean. I was an Airframes Aircraft Mechanic (Hydraulics). On this day, I was assigned to remove and replace an elevator actuator. It was in the hell hole area of the E2C Hawkeye aircraft. To get to it, I had to get my entire body inside the hell hole. The plane was located on the flight deck. I got inside and went to work. There were no flight operations at the time, so it was a perfect opportunity to get it done. I had just about finished installing the good actuator when I noticed the aircraft moving. The Yellow Shirts (Aircraft handlers) were backing the plane until the hell hole where I was, hung over the water. With me still inside of it completely over ocean water. You see, to make room on the flight deck of an Aircraft Carrier, the planes would be backed up until the tail end would be over the side of the ship.

There I was, stuck out into no man's land. I yelled

out, but no one heard me. I could not risk trying to show myself, because if I fell into the ocean, I may never have been found. It is also a known fact that Sharks followed Navy Ships since we dumped all our garbage in the ocean. This situation got more stressful as time went by. I started getting cramps, because of the cramped compartment I was waged into. If I eventually was found to be unaccounted for, the ship would go to a "Man Overboard," alert. Which would have changed the course of the ship to backtrack. The Helicopters would have been launched. All of this went through my mind. Slight desperation started to set in at this point. How long could I last, days, a week? They would find me when the plane was to fly. I could be killed easily by moving flight controls. Moving actuators, push-pull rods, or several other moving parts all around me. Then just like that, about two hours into my ordeal, someone heard me. They pulled the plane forward, and I was taken to sick bay. No damage was done, except to my psyche. I got over it and never took anything for granted again.

I had a 1974 Oldsmobile Cutlass that I called Suzzie Bell. I had two bikes, a Honda Interceptor 750, and a Yamaha FJ 1200. Lived in Downtown San Diego, CA. Was single and surrounded by unbelievably beautiful women. Life was particularly good for me. In my personal life and professionally as well as I was still in the US Navy. I had to be one of the happiest guys on the planet. One day, after work, I dressed up in my motorcycle gear and headed for home. While on a San Diego freeway, and only a few minutes away from my girlfriend's house. The last thing I remember was a car in front of me locking up its brakes. For no reason, this car slammed on its brakes and learned later what happened. I had to lay it (my motorcycle) down right there on the freeway. I was told that my bike just flipped over once. I, on the other hand, flipped head over heels many times. Thank God I had a helmet on. I woke up in a hospital bed with my girlfriend Kelli and my best friend Patrick at my bedside. I had no broken bones but did sustain a concussion. Bumps and bruises all over my body, but I was lucky. I could have been run over by another vehicle. I did not remember anything at the accident scene. How I didn't get more seriously injured or even killed, I'll never know. I was told later that the interstate was full of cars. I couldn't go around the vehicles that were stopping in front of me. Because there were vehicles on both sides of me when this happened. How both of the vehicles on either side of me were not involved is crazy luck and a miracle. I feel blessed not to have lost my life in this accident.

Glen and I walked home to my cousin's house in Houston again. Decided to take a shortcut and had no worries at all. A man came out of his front door, without us noticing him. He then gets our attention with a loud voice, hold it right there. We both froze as we turned to face the loud voice. He was pointing some kind of hunting rifle at us. How he could not see that we were just kids escapes me. The man scared us to tears. I thought we were going to die. Holding us at gunpoint as he yelled at us to stay out of his yard. His yard was not a fenced-in yard as it resembled an open field. He finally allowed us to leave at what seemed like hours to us. When this man said that he almost shot us, my knees almost buckled. I was so shaken up. I lost my appetite, no supper for me with my stomach in a knot.

I had an intense weightlifting regimen while in the Navy. It was four of us who worked out together. Six days a week no matter what we were all in the gym. One night we decided to meet up at a smoothie and protein drink shop. This place was in the suburban San Diego town of Linda Vista. A town known for its large Vietnamese population. In fact, the shop where we were headed was near a Vietnamese restaurant. Lex couldn't make it, so he went somewhere else. Patrick was to meet us there later. So, Rubio and I rode our motorcycles straight there. We parked our bikes and kind of hung out until Patrick arrived. Then four Vietnamese men came out of the restaurant and started staring at us. We heard them speak in their native language. Instead of going to their car, they came over to where we were. It was now obvious that they were all gang members. The leader did all the talking. He said, "Hey can I check out your Bikes," in a sarcastic tone. I could see that Rubio was getting that sardonic look in his eyes. Oh no! I figured there was no way to get out of fighting at this point. Been there, done that!

Rubio told him no! You can't check out our bikes. The leader came up to Rubio and tried to throw a punch. It missed its intended aim. That was the opening that Rubio was looking for. He caught the leader in the jar and again in his mouth with a combination left cross and a right hook. I yelled at the other three knuckleheads to stay out of it. Watching Rubio beat the leader rather well, and keeping the others out of it was my job. I figured this should wrap up quickly. I thought it did as the leader got into his car. He had enough so I thought. But wait a minute, he got back out of his car with what looked to be a small caliber handgun. The leader, having the upper hand now, became bolder. He walked up to Rubio and pointed the gun at his head. It looked like a slow-motion movie. One of the three I had in check punched me in my face. It felt like a girl slapped me, very weak. I told them I would punch all three of them if that happened again. The leader at this point was running behind Rubio threatening to shoot him. At some point I saw Patrick arrive, and so did the leader. On his way back to his car, he stops in front of me and points the gun at my forehead. My life flashed in front of my eyes. I stared straight into the leaders' eyes, a sight I thought would be my last. I guess they didn't know if Patrick had a gun or not. He did not have a gun but was a bodybuilder. He looked like Arnold Schwarzenegger next to them. As Patrick got out of the car, the four cowards jumped into their Honda Civic and sped away. This Leader guy was a punk in my opinion. Everyone with a gun knows that you never pull it unless you will be shooting it. His life was never in danger, so he had no reason to pull the gun in the first place. We all went into the smoothie place to have our protein drinks. Trying to calm Rubio down was the first order of business. I mean I had no doubt what Rubio was going to do to this leader punk. Rubio was bench pressing 405 pounds, so I mean really leader dude. Then the San Diego Police Department (SDPD) showed up to begin harassing us and threatening to arrest us for fighting. We explained to the Police what had happened, and they finally left. It was hard to get Rubio to calm down and the cops did not help at all. Looks like the leader and his gang of wimps were going to get away with it. Everyone rendezvouses at my place downtown to discuss this thing. Lex showed up with his gun. Patrick and I talked to Rubio and Lex about going back to Linda Vista. For one, I knew that there were real gangs in that neighborhood. I made sure everyone got home safely. Then I lay in bed all night, as my life continued to flash in front of me. I thought of my younger years and all the confusion. I remembered all the events that had happened that very night.

I once bought a pickup truck while still in high school. I was determined to pay for this vehicle as soon as possible. I got two jobs at fast food restaurants. Patrick and I worked at Kentucky Fried Chicken and Wendy's Old-Fashioned Hamburgers. Patrick and I ran to the kitchen at KFC. At Wendy's, it was a different situation there. Multiple shifts with different co-workers every workday. This one guy who thought he was better than everyone else, worked there too. He was supposed to be from a rich family. But his father wanted him to work to build his character. This guy was a pain in the neck. He was rude to everyone and a chump. In my opinion, I let him know how I felt about him. One night we were closing down together, and an argument started. Patrick was working next door at KFC and I were on his ride home. I go to leave to meet Patrick at my truck for the ride home. I may have gotten thirty feet away when I heard, hold it right there. Patrick reaches into my truck for my shotgun. I never went anywhere without my shotgun. I turned around to see the chump aiming a rifle at me. I could clearly see his finger on the trigger. That was not the thing that scared me the most. It was the anger in his eyes, an intense Aqua Blue.

They were undulated eyes with needle points for pupils. I froze so still in my tracks, like a statue in a museum. When he saw Patrick pull out my shotgun from my truck, he fled back into the restaurant. I never saw him again because he quit working at Wendy's immediately.

Claudia the kids and I arrived at Knotts Berry Farm amusement park. It was to be our first family vacation together. Two days of absolute fun and happiness. At the park, and the other at the water park. It was during this time that it began to happen. I started to get pain in my stomach. I also started to have swelling in my tongue, lips, hands, fingers, and worse my throat. I went to see an Allergist and immunologist who specialized in what I was experiencing. After the little mini vacation was over, I went back over the road on my big truck. The symptoms continue to increase in intensity. Especially the stomach pains. Which the doctor thought was my gallbladder in some way. I got set up for a CT scan, to rule out or affirm my Gallbladder. They gave me a solution to drink prior to taking the CT scan. I must have been allergic because I regurgitated all over the place. This irritated my throat, causing throat pain. They finished the CT scan, and Claudia and I took off to her parents' house. Just for a little visit, since I was scheduled to leave for work that night. At my wife's parents' house, I started to have difficulty breathing. Her mother gave me some Benadryl, which helps. It got so bad that I had to put my head back just to breathe. At this point, they must have deliberated on whether to call an ambulance or not.

They decided it would be quicker for Claudia to just drive me to the hospital. She scared the daylight out of me as she blew through red light after red light. I found out later that she probably saved my life by doing this wild driving. At the emergency room, they took me back to an examination room. I don't remember anything after I was brought back. My wife said that they wanted to perform a tracheostomy on me. She was in the emergency exam room with me. She wouldn't let them perform that procedure unless it was 100% necessary. I'm so glad that she did that. They hit me with the EpiPen shots 6 times total. Plus, she said that they had me on some powerful allergy meds intravenously. I was placed in (ICU) Intensive care unit for about a week. My condition was critical and was not improving until they finally found the problem. It was medication prescribed to me. They had been continuously giving me this medicine, which is why my condition would not improve. Once they stopped giving me that medicine, I returned to normal in a matter of days. I don't remember much of anything… my wife was my eyes and ears. I went home from the hospital an incredibly lucky man to still be alive. I was so fortunate that my wife never once left my side. While in ICU, I had visitors, but I don't remember them even being there.

My advice to everyone reading this is not to take medication for granted. Any time you get new meds, google them to find out the side effects and other information. I failed to do this, and just took the doctor's word. When I went back to my doctor, he seriously wanted me to continue taking the medication that almost killed me. I immediately replaced him with another doctor. Obviously, my doctor had been getting kickbacks from the pharmaceutical company. My life was not more important than bonus money. By the way, my throat was closed to the size of a needlepoint. How I survived that is amazement.

In October 2020, I found out that I had contracted the COVID-19 virus. Normally, I never ever get sick. I had gone thirty-plus years without getting sick. I never had the Flu or a Cold. My mom (grandmother) used natural remedies on me. I guess that had a positive effect on my health. But I caught COVID-19 and caught it bad. I moved to the guest room and my wife kept a close eye on me. The first four days, I did not eat anything. I also didn't get out of bed in those four days. I only got up when my wife made me. I couldn't even breathe very well, and the headaches were 24 hours a day. I could only walk halfway to the living room before I had to return to the guest room. I was ordered by my wife to move my arms when walking. She said it would help keep the fluid out of my lungs. At one point, I called all my children to let them know that I might not make it. I got to a point that the day might come when I might have to do the hospital thing if there was room for me. The ventilator was my very last resort. I knew lots of people who had died after being placed on a ventilator. This COVID-19 virus was the worst sickness I have ever had in my life. I don't want any parts of that again.

CHAPTER 26

PLACES I HAVE TRAVELED TO.

It's true that I have been to all fifty states. A dream of mine ever since I became a professional truck driver. I love the state of California since I believe it to be the best weather out of all the states. In California, you can go to the desert, and the mountain snow, and ride the waves at the beach all on the same day.

These friendliest states in the United States in my opinion. They are Wisconsin, Idaho, and Utah, not necessarily in that order. Milwaukee can be a little shaky sometimes. Idaho is full of friendly people all over that state. I love going there because of this fact. Utah is where I call home currently, so to encounter friendly people while I am active is normal. I love being amongst my fellow Utahans anytime I'm out. When I told people that I was moving to Utah, they warned me about the Mormons. It turned out that the Mormon people were not just nice, but super nice. They are good people and are never rude or obnoxious. Crime is super low, and Utah is a 2nd Amendment and Constitutional following state.

Montana is breathtakingly beautiful. I would recommend this state to anyone looking for nature's bonanza of adventure. Oregon and Washington are remarkably similar. I really do not get a really good vibe in Oregon, but it is very beautiful. Washington is a little better feeling. My oldest son loves Washington and the "Great Northwest." He likes all the outdoor activities available in this vast region. I don't like all of the rain, but Seattle is my personal favorite.

My home state (Louisiana) where I was born and raised has a special place in my heart. Unfortunately, I'll most likely never live there again. My childhood memories I still have of living in Louisiana are a double-edged sword. Many of it explained in this book, many are probably blocked out. All the deep family secrets will probably never be known or unsuppressed on purpose. I decided to not let that happen to my suppressed true story. On a positive note, Louisiana has great advantages for many industries. Oil Refineries and restaurants that is second to none. I've been to France and my home state is right there with France, in my opinion. Louisiana is truly a sportsmen's paradise! I may have left Louisiana seemingly for good. But Louisiana is still deeply rooted in me.

Hawaii changed very little through the years. I've been to Hawaii at least seven times. In the 1980's, I liked it more than the last time I was there, in 2016. I have done just about everything there. The best thing ever was the visit to the Pearl Harbor Memorial. That experience always leaves me with a hollow feeling. My advice for anyone's first visit to Hawaii is to do the cruise ship thing. This way you will see all the Islands and avoid Hotels and rental cars.

Illinois, Indiana, and Iowa all look pretty much the same. Except for the fact that Iowa is the corn-growing and Pork-producing state in the United States. I lived in the Chicagoland area for about a decade. Let's just say it was an eye-opening experience. Chicago is the king of many different ethnic restaurants. Down this one street in Kokomo, Indiana, a town just outside of Indianapolis. I had seen the most Buffet-style restaurants in one area. I had never seen so many in such a small area. In Iowa, it reminded me of my early years in Louisiana. Of all the dirt roads throughout the state of Iowa. I had lived on a dirt road for years, which they paved when I was in the military.

I have seen where the Mississippi River began, and where it ended. Also, every mile of it borders Minnesota, Wisconsin, Iowa, Illinois, Missouri, Kentucky, Tennessee, Mississippi, and Louisiana. Minnesota is one of the cleanest cities I have ever seen. It shows it in the city of Minneapolis, which I have always been impressed by. Minnesota is known for being very cold. In International Falls, Minnesota I have stood just feet from the Canadian Border. This city is the coldest spot in the lower 48 states.

People think of New York State as this robust extremely busy place.

Actually, most of the state of New York is countryside loaded with small townships. But down in New York City, it is chaos. Extremely expensive and crowded.

North Dakota and South Dakota are similar in many ways. Maybe South Dakota has a slight edge because of Mt Rushmore National Park. Also, the Black Hills where General Custer's last stance had taken place. North Dakota does have the final home of Laura Ingalls Wilder, the author that the TV show "Little House on the Prairie" was based on. North Carolina and South Carolina are different in my opinion. With North Carolina being big in the NASCAR Racing circuit. College Basketball is huge in North Carolina. This state is also known as the "First in Flight," by the Wright Brothers. Tobacco Production is a major industry as well in North Carolina. South Carolina has the famous Beaches and Golf courses. It was the first state to succeed from the Union, leading to the Civil War.

Rhode Island was a brief experience where I would only drive through it on my way to Boston Massachusetts. One thing is for sure about this state. It has a spectacular coastline, lined with seaside colonial towns.

Alabama has college football as its main attraction. This state is big in agriculture and southern hospitality. I have driven just about everywhere in Alabama. And through this state more often than anything.

I went to Alaska by way of a US Naval Ship. It was in the summertime…thank goodness. Where it was daylight all day except for one hour of darkness. In the winter, it is mostly dark, most of the time with only an hour of daylight. I visited Anchorage, Alaska and I recommend a visit there if possible. It has an adventure galore and unlimited picturesque views in every direction.

Arizona is the Grand Canyon state and my favorite place in this state is Flagstaff, Arizona. Phoenix is the largest city in Arizona. It is known as the "Valley of the Sun." The city of Prescott is known as a perfect retirement place to live since it has sunshine for a significant percentage of the year.

Arkansas is one of the main drives through the states. Driving through Northern Arkansas is very Beautiful. There are scenic mountains and hills everywhere. It is known as the 'Hill Country."

Denver Colorado has some of the most beautiful sights in the state. Both stationary sites and wild animals. The weather is not consistent, but I guess one could get used to it. The high altitude is real when your activity level increases. The Rocky Mountains are very majestic. It is a lovely place to visit at certain times of the year.

Connecticut, Massachusetts, New Hampshire, and Vermont all look pretty much Identical. In some cases, you must read road signs to see which one of these states you are in. My favorite of these states would have to be New Hampshire. No specific reason, only that I always got a better feeling in New Hampshire.

I've been all over Delaware many times and was not impressed. It is a tax-free state if that might entice anyone. Once while in Delaware on my way to Virginia Beach. I called myself taking a shortcut from the Turnpike toll road. Yikes! On the very southern border with Maryland and the Chesapeake Bay. Where Mr. Francis Scott was inspired by the Revolutionary War Battle. He wrote the Star-Spangled Banner. I Drove underneath the Chesapeake Bay through an underground / water tunnel. Evidently, the state of Virginia has a number of these underground and water tunnels. Maryland, Virginia, and Delaware are all very similar.

Florida has a lot of sunshine and hurricanes. It doesn't do a lot for me. Since I have become adapted to the West Coast. Which is dry heat with extraordinarily little humid weather. Florida is hot and very humid, and yes, I did grow up in that type of environment in Louisiana.

I liked Georgia for visiting only. But this state is like neighboring states like Alabama, South Carolina, and parts of Florida. Must mention the Peaches that are a thing in Georgia. Also, the home of well-known sports teams. Coca-Cola has its headquarters located.

You can be driving in the state of Kansas and get the feeling that it looks the same everywhere. Thank goodness for mile markers and GPSs.

Kentucky has the famous horse racing track at Church Hill Downs. The Kentucky Derby is the first leg of the Triple Crown. Kentucky has what might be the most beautiful horse-gracing land in the country.

The last state to complete my 50th state was Maine. My wife and I decided to drive from Allentown, Pennsylvania. Along with our youngest two kids, Paulina, and Cristian. We left my brother's wedding for Maine. It was a nice road trip. We celebrated as we drove across the New Hampshire and Maine border. Spent a night in Portland, Maine, and with that, I had completed my goal of being in all 50 states.

My favorite place in the state of Michigan is Detroit. I just get a good vibe about this city. You get easy access to Canada, and it is not far from Cleaveland and Chicago. Motown comes to mind both with the automobile industry and the music industry.

The state of Mississippi is familiar as it is a neighboring state to my native Louisiana. I have traveled a lot of miles in the state of Mississippi.

The Show Me state reminds me of all the cross-country road trips I have taken. I worked at two trucking companies in Missouri, Minnesota, Illinois, Arizona, Iowa, Washington, Ohio, and California. I don't ever get a good feeling in Missouri or Nebraska.

Nevada has been a state that I have visited a lot.

Both professionally and personally. I've gotten married in Las Vegas once and have been to other weddings there. My son was stationed near Reno, Nevada at one time. I visited him as much as I could. I have basically been all over Nevada.

This state is home to Yellowstone National Park. Wyoming is a very rough state weather-wise. It can and will get bad in the wintertime. Let's just say that Wyoming is a harsh environment as it pertains to foul weather, like windy conditions and snow. When I describe this state, I will express the beauty and wide openness. The rough landscape, and its notorious Cowboys and Rodeos.

I call this state the on-ramp state. For some odd reason in West Virginia, drivers don't know how to enter a freeway safely. They completely ignore the merge/yield signs never looking at the freeway traffic (which has the right of way). They enter the freeway as if they are the ones who have the right of way.

I never get a good feeling whenever I travel to the state of Nebraska. It is similar to Missouri.

All I have gotten from Northern New Jersey was pretty much loud mouths and bad attitudes. The beaches have beautiful areas to visit. Southern New Jersey is much friendlier.

In my opinion, the state of New Mexico is there to travel through it.

Although, I did eat what may be the best tasting

Burrito ever there. It was in Santa Fe, New Mexico, and from a food truck. Much of this state is uninhabited. This is probably why New Mexico was the birthplace of the nuclear bomb. The Roswell incident occurred in this state. One very unknown fact about New Mexico is that it was named before the country of Mexico was named.

This is a known fact amongst us truckers in Ohio. It is the most ticketed state. Even though it isn't one of the larger states like Alaska, California, and Texas. You would think that one of the larger states would produce more traffic citations. They (the state police) never hide to use entrapment techniques like many other states will do. No, Ohio State police will park their bright white police cruisers right in the center of the freeway. They use long-range lasers and will catch vehicles speeding long before they are seen. The Pro Football Hall of Fame is in Canton, Ohio. I've driven by this historic place many times.

Tornado Alley and the bible belt describe Oklahoma the best. Tulsa, Oklahoma is negatively known for one of the worst massacres in US history. It is known as the "Black Wall Street Massacre." Way back on May 31st to June 1st of 1921, is when this horrible thing occurred.

One of Pennsylvania's biggest deals is the "Little League World Series." The Keystone State is one that I have traveled all over. I've seen all of this state, plus many of its historical locations. I was in Pennsylvania just last year for my brother Rason's wedding. It looked the same as always.

Tennessee is my favorite state of mine. I have a taste for country music, and Nashville is the absolute place for that. Graceland, where Elvis left his stamp on Rock and roll is in Memphis, Tennessee. Memphis is famous for its barbecue Ribs. I've traveled the whole state as a truck driver.

Texas is big and everything about Texas is big. From its cowboy culture and ranching; to the longhorn cattle. Texas has more oil than any other Lower 48 state that I know of. Who knows how much Alaska has?

Texas has multiple Clements as well as geographical terrains. Every human being on earth could fit in the state of Texas with room to spare.

Washington DC was interesting as far as the National Mall is concerned. I love history and there is a lot there. I was disappointed in the (so-called) African American Museum. First, I do not identify myself as an African American because it is a label and not a people. Our ancestors had their names taken away, WHY? Second, our history didn't start with slavery. I will leave this here since I know a lot more about my history after researching books written prior to the 19th century.

One of the things I am proud of having been to all 50 states is sports venues. As a sports fan, I have seen driven by almost every major university in the United

States. I have also seen many of the professional sports stadiums too. Our country is exceptionally beautiful with so much to see and experience. I have seen most of the world by way of my time in the US Navy.

Japan was mostly more of a seen-it, without-stepping-on-it type of deal. I am good with that, and besides, one of my sons was stationed in Japan. As a Navy sailor onboard a United States Aircraft Carrier.

South Korea was interesting because of our US Army presence there. They of course were helping guard the border with North Korea. The people were nice there and very welcoming. There were Nike factories there, so I got myself a pair of sneakers. At a very discounted price…$10 (smile).

I went to Hong Kong when it was under British rule. The city was modern and clean. The Bay was full of Hydroplaning large sea vessels. It was a tremendous experience. I'm still kicking myself for not getting any China dinnerware sets made of porcelain. I figured I'd go back someday soon, and never did. And with China as the conqueror of Hong Kong these days, I probably will never set foot there again.

Singapore, which I visited many times, was literally crime-free. The punishment for crime was so severe, that nobody dared commit any crimes. It just wasn't a good idea to be a criminal in Singapore. For instance, a US President asked the leader of China how the sexual crimes were against China's children. The Chinese leader told him none because the punishment for any crimes against children was death.

There were lots of water sports available in the country of Thailand.

The food was awesome all over the city. Not a good place to seek prostitutes, if that's your thing. Because of disease and people walking around suspiciously in a not-so-normal way (couldn't tell what sex they were).

This was a dream come true. To be in Mombasa, Kenya on the east coast of Africa (a few times). I still need to get to the West African coast, where my DNA tells me how I came from there. Makes sense because most of the slaves taken on the Transatlantic Slave Trade came from Western Africa. On my first visit, I learned that there were still slave cages around. We asked the Africans if it would be wise to move there in Africa. They said definitely not, since we didn't belong there. They went on to say that their people helped capture us for the slave ships. We asked them who we were, and they said, "The people of the book" (The Bible). The word bible is not found anywhere in the Holy Scriptures. It took me years to process what these African men told us. I totally understand what they meant now.

Perth Australia was amazing to visit. Located on the western coast as it faces the Indian Ocean. For some reason, all the Afro-Americans were pursued aggressively by the Caucasian women. Let's just say that it was a port of call none of us would ever forget.

A couple of my shipmates and I went to a bar to have a beer. There were these older Australian men there. They had been in World War II representing Australia. They told us astonishing stories about fighting alongside the US Army (Those Bloody Yanks). As they put it, causing us to all laughed as we listened. The beer we were drinking was way stronger than what we were used to. I somehow insulted the chef, by asking that my steak be cooked well done. My steak was set in front of me basically burnt. The prices were reasonable, so I got my own hotel room. I was not big on hanging with a crowd. My hotel room would be considered a three-star hotel back in the States.

India, Greece, Canada, Italy, Egypt, and Saudi Arabia, all were places I was near, but never actually set foot on. "A stone's throw away" might explain it better.

I've been to Mexico many times. My wife is a Latina and has relatives both in Mexico and Spain.

Malaga Spain was an experience of a lifetime. I didn't know it then, but this city was used as a vacation destination for the Europeans. There were lots of evidence of the tribe of Juda (the children of Yisrael), and the Muslim Moors. Both of with occupied Spain and Portugal for over 800 years or up until the Christian Crusades were successful in driving the Moors out and enslaving Yisrael.

Cannes, France was a great port of call. My shipmate Fighter Lex and I ate Croissants while drinking fine Wine. It was educational and fun, filled with many activities.

We were given strict rules to follow while on ship to prepare us for Liberty in Karachi, Pakistan. We were told that this was a Muslim Nation with strict customs. No Alcohol or drugs were allowed. Do not eat anything not thoroughly cooked. Drink only bottled water with no ice. The first day on liberty we end up at a party with Alcohol and women for the taking! Money over religion, I guess. Many of the locals chewed on Opium, Yuck! I remember ordering fried fish and bottled water. I have seen other sailors eating from the salad bar and drinking out of cups with ice. Just what they told us not to do. I remember drinking a lot of Bourbon and being pretty drunk for the trip back to the ship. We traveled by way of liberty boats. Locals hired by the Navy to transport sailors to and from the ship. On the way back, I have no idea how I did not regurgitate. That night, all hell broke out, with sailors being sick from not following instructions on what not to eat or drink. Guys were running to the Head (restroom) with diarrhea. Some made it, and some did not make it. All I know is that we used this opportunity to place bets on who made it and who didn't. Sounds cruel but it was their own fault might as well capitalize. One guy never made it out of his rank, so gross to witness that.

Subic Bay, Philippines is now the ex-Navy base and airfield. Not far from Manila but strategically located. I lost count of how many times I was there in Subic Bay. My biggest memory there in the Philippines was how I learned all about sex. Most sailors went to bars and paid the bar fine for these girls. Then they would go home with them and have sex. The Clap Line (Sailors who had contracted a venereal disease) would be exceedingly long. I have never been in that line, thanks to Paula, a Filipino woman (older than I). She taught me all about sex and how not to get sexual diseases. Every time we went to the Philippines, Paula would be there on the pier waiting for me. One of the places we hung out at was this Soul Food restaurant. This Afro-American lived there, and it was the restaurant. Tattoos were big there in Subic Bay as well as tailored clothes (buyer beware). One thing I noticed was that the music in the clubs was like five years or more behind the USA.

CHAPTER 27

THE WOMEN IN MY LIFE

Claudia

I've been involved with many women in my life. I only recognized those that were serious. Also, those that were special in my past. I'm not proud of my philandering around with women while in the Navy. I'm talking about fraternizing in a way that's not in a gentlemanly manner. I'm not proud of it, at all, but it did happen with women all over the world, including the good old USA. I'll work through these women from today back. From my awesome wife (who is my queen and is above any past relationship) to my first girlfriend. But even my wife was once my girlfriend.

My wife, Claudia Alexander is the best one of them all…thank goodness! I saved the best for last, and I really mean last. She is my soul mate, best friend, lover, and much more. Claudia is Mexican with an authentic look of beauty. Not too far removed from Spain, with her paternal side still having cousins in Spain. She has been mistakenly thought to be from many different nationalities. She is often taken as a Caucasian, even by native Mexicans. Claudia is the best thing to ever have happened to me. I am a lucky man to have been picked by her. She is submissive and very devoted and worthy of me treating her as my queen and I as her King. Her parents treat me as their son, and it is very much appreciated by me. I am close to both her brother and her sister. Claudia may look Caucasian, but is most definitely not, she is 100% Latina.

When I dropped religion out of my life, it was a strain on our relationship. She is such a strong woman and so in love with me, we got through it with time. I have so much respect for how she handled such a drastic move on my part. Claudia is generous and is an extremely good person. She is my wife, but she is my best friend and soulmate first.

Laura

Laura came along in my life at a vulnerable period. I was in the middle of a divorce with Kelli. Laura was a descendant of Russian Jews. She was a Caucasian woman with blonde hair, and green eyes, and a gymnastics athlete. Laura had two beautiful mulatto girls that I truly miss. What Laura and I had was a highly intense sexual relationship. Marriage was floated around but was probably never seriously going to happen.

Laura moved into my home, mainly because she told me that she was pregnant with my child. Even though I was under the impression that she had gotten a Tubal Ligation (tubes tied). She assured me that sometimes it was possible. She ended up not being pregnant and our relationship fizzled.

Juanita

Juanita was an Afro-American full of life. She was also coming out of an abusive marriage as I was. So, we were both on the rebound. Laura and I had broken up briefly and I started dating Juanita. Who was a person that was a particularly good person? We dated briefly, but her roots were in Chicago, and I knew that eventually, I would be moving back to San Diego, California. Juanita was too good of a person to try and uproot her. I felt awful about how I ended things with her. I pray that Juanita finds true love.

Kelli

Kelli was my first wife. We were married for nineteen years. We raised our three children together. I still don't understand what, "Irreconcilable Differences," means to this day. That is what I was accused of anyway. I must thank Kelli for leaving me because it allowed me to find my true love (Claudia Mercedes). But all I know is that one day she said she was leaving. Then she was gone, and I moved on. I have forgiven her since that is what we are called to do. My life with Kelli was a fog. I've long since let go of it for whatever it was worth. Kelli was Caucasian and that didn't matter in my opinion. We are all human beings after all. I should have known better when she proposed to marry me. Isn't that supposed to be the man's thing? It did not work, but I do not wish any negative vibes on her. It wasn't meant to be evidently.

Lisa

Lisa was one of the women I treated wrong in how it ended. She was a Mexican with Green eyes and nothing but genuinely nice to me. I know I dated or been with a lot of women with green eyes. Trust me, it was all just coincidental. My wife Claudia has green eyes but hers are way more beautiful than the others. I used to wonder what would have happened if I had chosen Lisa over Kelli. No, on the other hand, Lisa's father hated Afro-Americans period. We dated in secret and that right there means it never would have worked. She loved her father to the moon and back. I would never come between her and her racist father. Anyway, I was kind of dating them both at the same time. I know how distasteful that sounds, but I was only having sex with Lisa. I quit seeing Lisa unceremoniously, something I should not have done like that. She was good to me, and I was an ASS!

Bree

My nineteen-year-old girlfriend... talk about robbing the cradle. I was twenty-six years old at the time. A motorcycle-riding dude, without a care in the world. How we met was unorthodox for sure. While visiting with one of Patrick's girlfriends. He and I were seated on a couch talking. Then this girl came in and sat right next to me. I could tell that she was young right away. She told me that her name was Bree, and she was very straightforward. I told her my age and that I was a full-grown man, she got even more interested in me. She told me that she was only nineteen years old. She said that older men were her preference. Keep in mind that all this is going on after just meeting for the first time. Suddenly, this young guy comes in and starts nervously looking around. I asked Bree who he was, and she said that he was her boyfriend. Before I could answer that, she said out loud "I want to go out with you." The poor guy left, and Bree and I started a relationship. In the end, I made her promise to find someone closer to her age. I was about to hook up with another woman. It was a smooth ending for Bree and me. Bree was a Caucasian young woman with brown hair and very blue eyes. I am sure she had no problem finding a replacement. It was fun while it lasted.

Laila

Job Core Girl was a chance meeting in another country. Even though both of us were from the USA. Patrick, Rubio, and I were walking around in Tijuana, Mexico. Just across the border with San Diego, California. The three of us are just chilling out as we check out the scene. When suddenly I heard this woman's voice directed at me. It was a beautiful Afro-American signaling me over to her. She tells me that she wanted to get to know me. I asked her were she always so straightforward. I took down her phone number since cell phones hadn't been invented yet. It was a pager, a phone boot, or the good old landline. Her name was Laila, an African name that I thought was interesting. She was incredibly good-looking, and her skin tone was very uniquely deep brown with zero blemishes. Her hair was braided professionally, and she had intensely beautiful deep brown eyes. Laila spent lots of time at my apartment. She was an excellent cook and lover.

Things started going south when she wanted me to meet her parents. I was not ready for that at all. Then she decided to show her displeasure with my decision. She called herself to go off on me in front of my friends. Patrick, Lex, Rubio, Ron, and I were planning a trip to Los Angeles…to go to the party.

Laila let me know that she was going with us (with a bunch of Dude… really though). When I said no, that's when she went off on me in front of everybody. Our relationship ended that very night.

Doloris

Doloris was one that I thought would be the perfect woman for me.

She was an incredibly beautiful Afro-American woman. She was from Lake Charles, Louisiana (near my hometown). She wore her hair in a natural Afro and her body was perfect. Her smile was sweet and innocent, but her sense of humor was very above average. While on leave from the US Navy, I proposed to her, after a romantic dinner date. She flat-out said no and wouldn't even look at the engagement ring. I was so in shock; that I went back to California in a daze. She explained why she turned me down; her mother was her priority. Keep in mind that we were the same age, 28 years old. I was ready and she was not. I had to accept her taking care of her mother without any hesitation. We faded out of any type of relationship, especially since I was married to Kelli a year later. I respected Dolores for her decision not to marry me. Sometimes things are just not meant to be.

Deedee

Right after Doloris dumped me, I met someone else. Her name was Deedee, and she was an Afro-American.

For a short woman (I was 6'6") she was extremely good in bed. I mention this only because it was noteworthy. Especially since I had been with women all over the world. This was a rebound relationship and nothing else. I needed more than great sex, I needed to find the right life partner.

Katrina

My first official girlfriend's name was Katrina, who went to the same school as I did. I was in the 9th grade, and she was an 8th grader. Katrina was an Afro-American and nothing but great to me. Her mother laid down the law to me about sex, and I was a big-time virgin. No sex with my daughter (Katrina), no matter what. Not that sex was even on my mind at all, I do understand that it was a possibility. One night while hanging out at a party my sister Paula was giving. My girlfriend would not be arriving until later that night. Here comes Lavinia, like a straight line to me. I didn't know this at the time, but Lavinia was trying to break Katrina and me up. Lavinia and I sat on our telephone loveseat-looking thing. We talked for a while, then she started seducing me. Which I allowed like a dummy; being that I was committed to Katrina, who was much nicer. Lavinia and I started kissing at first, then we ended up in my sister's bedroom. Clothes were removed and on the bed we went. I of course had no idea what to do, and neither did she. I don't think

Lavinia knew what she was doing either. There we were, going at it without accomplishing anything. The reality of this encounter was that we never had had intercourse. We both left that bedroom still as virgins. Katrina showed up and we sat together. That was my opportunity to come clean and tell her what had happened. I did not do that as I would regret it later that week. I felt so ashamed to have committed this terrible sin against her. Lavinia couldn't wait to tell Katrina what had happened. Conveniently leaving out the fact that nothing sexually occurred intercourse-wise. This led to Katrina calling me up to let me know that she was quitting me. In a way, I was relieved. I caught up with Lavinia after school and tried to make her my girlfriend, but she denied me as if I was the plague. I was not the injured party, it was Katrina. Lavinia knew exactly what she was doing, breaking up my relationship with Katrina. With a lot of help from me, I am a willing participant. I was just a knucklehead caught up in a game of female trickery. I look at this whole experience like this. I almost made the worst mistake of taking a young girl's virginity away. And losing mine in the process. I learned from this event to never take anyone's virginity away. It was never the same between myself and girls from that moment and all the way through my high school years. I lost my virginity in the US Navy in Tijuana, Mexico.

Paula

I did not truly learn about sex until I went to the Philippines. By way of the United States Navy. I met a woman named Paula there. Who taught me everything about sex. It's weird how she has the same name as my half-sister Paula. Sailors were going around with all these different women. I stayed with only one woman, Paula. As a result, I never caught any venereal diseases. We called it the Clap line onboard ship, as they waited to be treated for sexual diseases. No smiles in this line and worse, no liberty if you find yourself in this line. Paula protected me from ever being in the vaunted "Clap Line." I was very aware of her taking care of me in that way. Therefore, I am grateful to her for everything she taught me. She benefited as well because I took very good care of her financially.

MY FAMILY TREE

First, I embrace my French Creole heritage. It comes from both my Paternal and Maternal sides of my family. With that being said, I do understand that my family's name and language were taken away. Leaving us with these slave names. We as a people, according to the Holy Scriptures, are still under the same curses as our ancestors. As it is written in the book of Deuteronomy chapter 28 verses 15 through 68:

1. Slavery and Captivity 28: 41, 49-50, 68
2. Having no power to stand against thy enemies 28: 25, 65.
3. Sent back to Mizrahim (Egypt) again by ships 28: 68.
4. Exiled in the land of their enemies 28: 25.
5. Scattered among all nations 28: 25, 64.

6. A very sick and diseased stricken people 28: 21-22, 25, 27, 59-61

7. At the bottom socially with other races high above them 28: 36, 43

8. Lost the true knowledge of who they are and will be called by many scornful nicknames other than Israel (Yisrael) and Hebrew 28: 37

9. Packed into prisons and jails 28: 48.

10. A non-Prosperous people 28: 17-20, 23-24, 29-31, 33, 38-41, 44,

11. An oppressed people by their enemies 28: 25, 48 12.Very religious and members of all religions 28: 36, 64

Deuteronomy 28

Verse 16- Cursed in the city = ghettos Cursed in the field = slave fields

Verse 21- Pestilence = Sexually transmitted diseases, diseases, etc. Verse 23- Brass & iron = chains…

Verse 26- Carcass will be meat = lynchings

Verse 29- Only be oppressed & spoiled. Verse 30- Another man will lay with your wife.

-You will build homes you will not live in Verse 31- You will be given to your Enemies.

Verse 32- Sons & Daughters given to others.

-You will not be able to save them Verse 34- You will be mad = Slavery

Verse 36- Brought to another nation.

Verse 38- You will work hard & gather little. Verse 41- Children shall go in captivity.

Verse 43- Strangers will go up and you will go down. Verse 45- You will be destroyed.

Verse 48- Yoke of iron on thy neck = slavery Verse 49- Eagle nation will come against you. Verse 54- You will hate your brother.

Verse 68- The Elohim (Lord) will bring you into Egypt (meaning bondage or Egypt = slavery because you don't need ships to go to Egypt for Negro-land in West Africa). Exodus 20: 2, You will be sold as Bondmen & bondwomen = into slavery.

I found it important to explain what my ancestors went through and who we are as a people. No other race/nation of people ever went through these curses in the book of Deuteronomy chapter 28: 16-68, but my people. Afro-Americans throughout the world don't know who they are. We are called only by bywords in place of our true identities. As it was written, it simply means that the curse is still going on to this very day. I smile to myself when I hear that my race/nation is referred to as a minority. Actually, we are not the minority since my people are spread throughout the entire world.

My paternal grandfather, Rev. Joeseph Ford, was a Baptist preacher and Sharecropper (farmer). He built three churches in Lake Charles, Louisiana, and at least one in Marksville, Louisiana. Before relocating from

Marksville to Lake Charles in the early 1900s. Saint Mary Baptist Church (Marksville) and in (Lake Charles) Saint John Baptist Church, Old Saint Mary Baptist now known as Hillcrest Baptist Church. Where my Uncle Earnest pastored for over 40 years before he retired as Pastor. Joe Ford supported his family by being a Sharecropper in the Lake Charles area. He was offered a Plantation style home to move his family into. This home was owned by the Landowner for which he was Sharecropping.

There was trouble from the local Caucasian men because of the fancy home my grandfather Joe and his family lived in. I don't know how long this trouble lasted. I do know that he would have his family sleep on the floor, for safety reasons. There were rocks thrown through the windows and up against the house itself. This was an effort to scare them off the property completely. To protect his family, Joe would climb up into a tree with his three single-shot muzzle load single shot type rifles. This is how he had to guard his family from any potential harm. Eventually, they left him and his family alone, especially since Joe was known to be a very good shot.

My paternal grandmother, Cemonia Ford as I was told, was a light-skinned beautiful woman. She had fine-graded hair which ran down her back. Cemonia was known to be a beautiful spirit as well. My sister Tesha supposedly, looks exactly like our beloved grandma Cemonia.

My grandfather's first language was Creole and did not speak English well. I've heard that he also spoke a little Hebrew. I'll just let that sit for a moment. I believe this fits in perfectly with my way of thinking. Meaning, where my ancestors came from, and who they were. All the children in my grandparents' house spoke Creole as their first language. They did not speak English until they started going to Grammar school. They went to a one-room schoolhouse for Afro-Americans only. It was deep into the "Jim Crow" era. This one-room school was located right down the street from where my cousins Sherrell and Uncle Earnest live today. There is a Walgreens store sitting where the little school once was. My Uncle Earnest, Aunt Mary, and Aunt Martha were the only ones to finish high school. My father Lester Ford was raised near where this school was once located, in the Prien Lake area of Lake Charles. My Uncle Earnest is the only surviving sibling out of all his sisters and brothers.' He actually lived in that large six-bedroom Plantation style home. With its wrap-around porch. They all worked on this share-cropping property of approximately one hundred acres of farmland. I would have loved to have seen this house that held so much of my family's history.

My grandfather's mold of transportation was a horse and buggy. Which ultimately was blamed for my grandmother Cemonia having four miscarriages. Eventually, my grandpa Joe got an automobile... problem solved. Joe and Cemonia had fourteen living children besides the four children who died before birth. My grandfather relocated with his brother (my great Uncle) Louis Ford. Uncle Louis's children's names were Raleigh, Lillian, and Diverson. The names of Joe Ford's children were Marietha, Emmett, Stephen, Joe, Almatine, Earnest, Ezekial, Shelton, Willie, Oscar, Jimmy, Bob (my dad), Mary, and Martha.

<u>My Grandfather -</u> Rev. Joseph Ford (1874-1978) <u>My Dad</u> - Lester "Bob" Ford (1930 - 1990)

<u>Me</u> - Marvin Alexander (1961 - present) <u>My Uncle</u> - Earnest Ford (1920 – present) <u>My Great Uncle –</u> <u>Louis Ford (? - ?)</u>

<u>My Grandmother –</u> Cemonia Ledoux Johnson (1890 -?) <u>My Great Grandfather</u> – Joseph Johnson (1869 -?) from Kentucky; the father of Cemonia

<u>My Great Great Grandmother</u> – Hester Roberson (?) mother of Joseph Johnson

<u>My Great Great Grandfather</u> – no name

<u>My Great Grandmother</u> – Ermontive Ledoux (?); from Georgia the mother of Cemonia

<u>My Great Great Grandmother</u> – Mary Ledoux (?); from Georgia

The Grandmother of Cemonia

Sadly, I don't know a lot about my father. I have picked up things from my Ford family members. Both my father and I both drank our coffee black. We both drove trucks for a living. We both served in the US Navy. I was in peacetime and my father was in the Korean War. My brother and others said that I look just like my father in appearance. I learned that my dad talked about me a lot from time to time. He knew exactly who I was. I am just grateful for anything that I can grab onto of him really. Rest in Peace Dad.

My birthmother's side of my family goes all the way back to France. A man that I only know as Landry (in English) and Landrodeaux (in French). He (Landrodeaux , a French citizen) relocated to Louisiana and bought land. This land is still in my family's possession today. I would spend several summers there, in what was called "Buck-Bayou." I learned many interesting things during my visits to Buck- Bayou. Like how to make homemade Ice Cream. How to make corn meal by hand, on a corn grinder type of apparatus. There were many acres of land, which was clearly enough to sustain enough crops to live on. Buck-Bayou is in the town of Palmetto, Louisiana, not far from the city of Opelousas. One of the stories about Buck Bayou was how Union Soldiers cut down a large tree to cross over the Bayou below. This was during the Civil War years.

Mr. Landrodeaux the Frenchmen was my mom/grandmother (Evelyn King Jack) distant grandparent. My mom's maiden name of course was Landrodeaux. My Great-grandmother Ophelia (Mom-Yah) had a maiden name of Thomas or Thompson. "MomYah" had five daughters. One of which was my mom. They were Aunt "Tee Fee" (Florance), Aunt Baybay, Aunt Mie, my mom Evelyn, and Aunt Lavene.

My fraternal Grandfather was Hilman King. My

birth mother (Melba), father, and my grandfather. I met him every now and then, but not very often. My Grandfather was a Sharecropper just as my other Grandfather was.

My mom had four girls and two boys, with only two still living.

My birth mother and my uncle Alcide Jack II. Evelyn's children were as follows: Aunt Bernadine, Aunt Florence, Aunt Dorothy, Melba (my birthmother, Uncle Alcide Jack II, and Uncle Herbert Jack.

My Great Grandmother, MomYah was born in 1877. I remember when she moved in with us. I oversaw keeping her company and making sure she had drinking water. I can also remember once when MomYah got too close to the gas heater (which had open flames). Her dress caught on fire and luckily for her, the adults were there to put it out. She was not injured thank goodness, and all was fine after that scare. MomYah only spoke Creole French, so it was hard to communicate with her. We made it work anyway somehow. I was able to pick up on some French, but not enough, unfortunately. For some reason, my generation was not taught our native Louisiana Creole language. We were told that if they taught us Creole French, we would probably be laughed at. A Generation before me; my father and all my aunts and uncles spoke Creole French as a first language. They would learn English once they went to school. Many Mexican Americans do it this way.

Spanish as a first language and English as a second. My wife is Mexican, and her first language is Spanish. The same goes for her kids, and so on. I wish I could have been lucky enough to have learned Creole French as my father before I had spoken.

MomYah is buried next to my mom. She passed away at the age of 96 years old. My mom was only 62 years old when she left this world.

CHAPTER 29

MY VEHICLES

<u>These are the vehicles I have owned:</u>

1. 1972 Ford Maverick 1972 Ford F-100 Pickup 1976 Toyota Corolla
2. 1973 Cadillac Eldorado 1978 Pontiac Grand AM 1985 Pontiac Sunbird
3. 1961 Chevrolet Pickup
4. 1974 Oldsmobile Cutlass
5. 1986 Honda Interceptor
6. 1987 Yamaha FJ1200
7. 1984 Ford Tempo 1989 Ford Escort Sport 1990 Ford Tempo
8. 1985 Chevrolet Station Wagon 1985 Nissan Sentra

9. 1984 Dodge Caravan 1991 Ford Ranger Pickup
10. 2004 Dodge Caravan
11. 1997 Ford Escort 1996 Chevrolet Lumina APV
12. 1995 dodge Caravan 1998 Ford f-150 Pickup 2003 Toyota Camry
13. 2006 Toyota Sienna
14. 2009 Chevrolet Cobalt 2004 Ford F-150 Pickup 2005 Ford Ranger Pickup 2004 Lincoln Navigator
15. 2012 Toyota Camry 2013 Ford F-150 Pickup 2009 Volkswagen Jetta
16. 2004 Ford Freestyle 2017 Ford F-150 Pickup 2020 Toyota Rav4

CHAPTER 30
I'M AT PEACE!

I Truly feel totally at peace with my past. I have let all of it go like "Water off a duck's back." I've learned to live in the present and not in the future or the past. We can prepare for the future but cannot predict it perfectly. I have also learned to only worry about the things that I can control. This makes for much less stress in my life.

I totally have forgiven my birthmother one hundred percent. She had a rough life and thanks to my mom, I did not have to be raised by her my whole life. My birth mother is who she is, and I am okay with that.

Therefore, I can't sit here and judge her when I am not perfect. Melba (my birth mother) is a child of God, and it is he who will judge us all. Melba and I talk all the time and keep it positive. I never bring up the subject of my father to her anymore. What is the use in that, with nothing to be gained?

We both talk about Bible verses and keep our conversations without anything negative. Even though she and I have had a disagreeable past. With that being said, we still had an operational relationship throughout my adult life. I think she may have liked me (not loved) and even cared about me as time went on. But allowing me to know who my father was just isn't going to happen. Sad!

I am very happily married to my best friend, who fulfills me in every way. Claudia is submissive to me and is the glue in our relationship. I treat her like the queen that she is, in my eyes. She treats me like her king. This has led to a successful marriage. She is perfect for me and I am for her.

Coming from totally different customs and family dynamics. She is Mexican, and my being an Afro-American never had a negative effect on our union. I've been with different women all over the world. What I come to realize is that we are all just human beings. A female is a female, and a male is a male.

I met both of my younger siblings at our brother Freddy's funeral. I went to Houston, Texas with my youngest son Cristian. We went straight to my brother Larry's house. There is where I met my little brother Rason for the first time. Larry addressed him as our brother. I was in shock as I stood there looking at him. The more we talked, the more it became evident that he and I were indeed brothers.

At the church, after the funeral, I met my little sister Tesha. It was emotional and fantastic at the same time. She was driven there by Dwight. I found out that he was my first cousin. I've since spent countless hours on phone conversations with Dwight. I have found out a plethora of information about family on my father's side. I met Brenda, Rason, and Tesha's mother. She told me things that completely confirmed who my father was.

Brenda was married to my father.

While attending my oldest brother Larry's funeral, I met two more first cousins.' Sherrell and Debbra, who was very gracious in inviting my wife and me to their home. They are the daughters of my father's brother, Uncle Ernest. My Uncle Ernest said when he saw me for the first time. "That is Bob's son." That was so surreal to hear him say that. It was a great visit with them, one that I will never forget.

Attending my brother's wedding was a positive experience. Rason and Jessie made the perfect bride and groom. My wife and our two youngest kids made a road trip out of it. Once the wedding was over, we hit the road for our adventure. Driving through Virginia, Maryland, Pennsylvania, Washington DC, New York, Massachusetts, Connecticut, New Hampshire, and Maine. We bonded on this trip and became even closer as a family.

I do not look back anymore. I live my life by being

grateful for being here. I'm writing this book because I want this story to get out. For just by chance, it helps someone in a similar predicament that I experienced. Like dealing with lies and deception. To know that after all, the truth will set you free. Be a forward thinker and a critical thinker and stay out of the past. I did everything in my power to make this book factual, truthful, and without lies. It is my perception, as I witness all the accounts that are written in this book. If someone in my family does not agree with the truth that I have presented in this book, I can only say, "By Your Leave Sir or Ma'am."

In the coming years as I prepare for retirement, I will enjoy the activities that I love. It will be big games, fishing, playing golf, umpiring baseball games, reading, pumping irons in the gym, and of course writing more books. Never thought I'd become an Author, but here I am. I think everyone should write their memoir. Whether you publish it or not is not the important thing here. It is like therapy when you dove into your past. It was definitely like therapy to write this book. Things that had been blocked out were unlocked or released out of my subconscious. It was as though I sat on the couch of a psychiatrist. In other words, this was an extremely positive experience. It is quite easy to author a book and have it printed in book form by a print shop. That way your story could stay private.

Unfortunately, my situation must be public because

of all the lies and Today, I enjoy observing my children succeed in whatever they have chosen to do in life. Also, enjoy every day with my loving wife and our Golden Doodle "Lucy."

<u>**Rest in Peace:**</u>

Whitney Alexander
Evelyn Jack
Aunt Florence
Aunt Bernadine
Aunt Dorothy
Alcide Jack I
Lester "Bob" Ford
Deborah Cutchin
Larry Ford
Joseph "Billy" Alexander
Ophelia "MomYah"
Aunt TeeFee

ACKNOWLEDGEMENT

I would like to thank:

Claudia Esquer Alexander